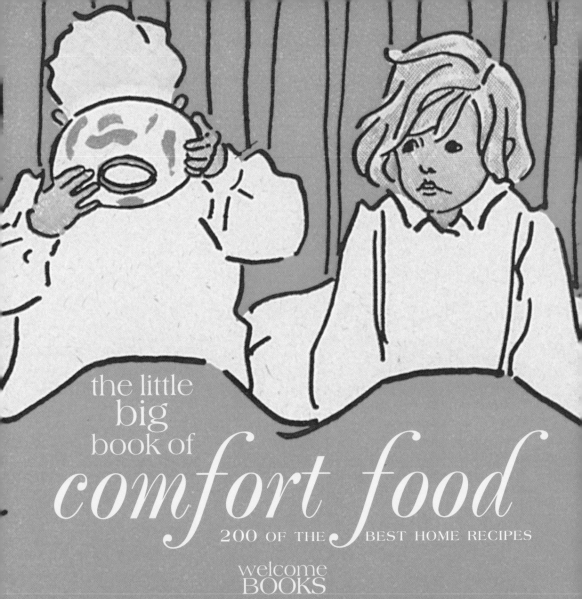

the little
big
book of

comfort food

200 OF THE BEST HOME RECIPES

welcome
BOOKS

NEW YORK · SAN FRANCISCO

contents

sides

beverages

foreword

What is it about a slice of toasted bread with butter and honey that warms my belly, settles my mind, and raises my spirits? The answer is so simple. It's what my Nana gave me when I was little and I was sick. And with that first bite, it takes me back there and holds me as tightly as she did. It's the same reason my youngest daughter, Katrina, reaches for a bowl of rice pudding when her heart is aching, or my oldest daughter, Natasha, craves chicken noodle soup when her sniffles seek relief. Each of us carries inside a special store of collected recipes that can be called upon when we are in need or want—to keep us company, to satisfy our souls, and to offer us comfort.

I have been baking and cooking for as long as I can remember. I used to sneak into the kitchen for pieces of gingerbread cookie dough, and my Nana would say she was going to name a cookie after me—"Lena Sneaka" (which means "Lena sneaks a peek"). But instead she gave me a few cookie cutters and my own little ball of dough to work with. Years later, when my daughters were growing up, we used to have as many as a dozen friends pile into our home to decorate hundreds of gingerbread and sugar cookies every year on the weekend before Christmas.

I love cooking with my daughters and never care if I am the sous chef or the cook. I want to make food swiftly and easily. I am not likely to spend the whole day in the kitchen, but I am also not interested at all in eating anything that it is not delicious.

You will find really simple, really good food in this cookbook. Over the years, my most

foreword

important lesson (outside of making gravy!) has been to buy organic (including chickens) and fresh ingredients whenever I can. I have few canned goods in my kitchen and I wish I had none. I don't want my family or my friends ingesting hormones, chemicals or genetically modified ingredients. I know it is a more expensive way to eat, but I am convinced the medical savings (later) will be huge. Reduce the sodas and the corn chips and the processed cheese.

If you are going to eat carbohydrates, stick to the ones in this book. Our Mama's Bread is truly wholesome and divine, warm for breakfast with raspberry jam or honey and sublime at Thanksgiving packed with turkey and stuffing and cranberries.

This cookbook is our tribute to those foods that have brought us pleasure, coziness, and companionship throughout our lives. We pooled together our personal recipe boxes along with those belonging to countless family, friends, and friends of friends, to create a cookbook that is bursting with comfort. Though we each have our own variety of personal favorites, there is an indefinable commonality among those meals we all find most consoling. And if, for shame, we've missed a special favorite of yours, please don't hesitate to write us and send the recipe along.

Enjoy. And watch the initials that sometimes follow the introductions. They will match to me (LT) or one of my daughters (KF or NTF).

—Lena Tabori

BREAKFAST

PERFECT SCRAMBLED EGGS

SERVES 1

To make perfect scrambled eggs you need a few basic tools and techniques, the most essential of which is low heat. Good butter and fresh eggs from free-range chickens are also important.

INGREDIENTS
1 tablespoon butter
2 eggs
1 tablespoon cream,
    half-and-half, or water
Salt and pepper

1. Heat an 8-inch nonstick frying pan over low heat. Add the butter.

2. Break the eggs into a small bowl. Add the cream, half-and-half, or water, and whisk with a fork until the yolks and whites are mixed.

3. When the butter has melted, pour the eggs into the frying pan and push the eggs around the pan with a rubber spatula so that uncooked portions run beneath the coagulating egg. Sprinkle with salt and pepper at this point.

4. Take the eggs off the heat before they are completely cooked, as they will continue to cook for a few seconds. Serve on a warmed plate, with toast.

Variations: Add crumbled bacon, a few tablespoons of chopped ham, fresh herbs such as basil, chives, tarragon, or parsley, or ¼ cup grated or crumbled cheese as the eggs finish cooking.

BAKED EGGS

SERVES 2

To bake—or "shirr"—an egg simply means you are baking an egg without its shell, typically in a small ramekin. It is a convenient way to serve eggs to a crowd. If you don't have ramekins, you can use buttered muffin tins.

INGREDIENTS
2 eggs
1 teaspoon butter
4 teaspoons heavy cream
Salt and pepper
Crumbled crisp bacon,
  or fresh herbs (optional)

1. Preheat the oven to 325 degrees.

2. Place a ramekin for each egg onto a sheet pan. Put a teaspoon of butter into each ramekin. Place the sheet pan with the ramekins into the oven, until the butter melts.

3. Break an egg into each ramekin, and pour 2 teaspoons of cream over each. Sprinkle with salt and pepper. If you wish, you may add fresh herbs (fresh tarragon is particularly good with eggs) or a teaspoon of crumbled bacon in the bottom of the ramekin before adding the egg.

4. Bake for 12 minutes, or until the eggs are just set. Serve immediately, with toast.

CLASSIC OMELET

SERVES 1

A great omelet requires a hot pan. Best of all is a well-seasoned black steel or old cast-iron frying pan that has never seen a drop of dish detergent. Eight inches is the proper diameter.

INGREDIENTS
2 large or extra-large eggs
Salt and pepper to taste
2 teaspoons butter

1. Crack the 2 eggs into a small bowl with salt and pepper to taste. Whisk thoroughly with a fork until the yolks and whites are blended.

2. Put an 8-inch nonstick skillet over high heat. Add the butter and swirl to coat the bottom of the pan. Heat until it's foaming, but do not let the butter brown.

3. Pour the eggs into the pan and let them cook, undisturbed, for just a few seconds, then shake the pan back and forth a bit to be sure your omelet isn't sticking.

4. Using a rubber or plastic spatula, lift the outside edges of the omelet up toward the middle and let the uncooked egg run underneath, onto the hot pan.

5. In less than half a minute, the omelet will be ready to fold over onto itself. The center will still be moist and creamy. Tilt the pan slightly to get the

CLASSIC OMELET

round sheet of eggs toward one side of the pan,
then use the spatula to fold half of the omelet over
the other half.

6. Slide omelet onto a plate and serve immediately.

Variations: If you want to fill an omelet, just make sure
that you don't overdo it (use 4 tablespoons of any filling, at most), and don't use anything too wet. Sprinkle
or spread it over the omelet before you fold it over
onto itself.

A few suggestions:
· ¹/₄ cup crisp crumbled bacon or diced ham.
· Thin slices of smoked salmon.
· A few tablespoons of mixed fresh herbs.
· Grated hard cheese of any type, or a smear
  of fresh goat cheese.
· A few tablespoon of any cooked vegetable
  you like, chopped.
· A drizzle of red or green salsa, at room
  temperature or warmed.

HUEVOS RANCHEROS

SERVES 4

Huevos Rancheros, or "rancher's eggs," is an extremely popular dish in Mexico, where eggs are eaten for most any meal. Our neighbors to the south brought their spicy egg dishes to California where they are enjoyed burrito style, with salsas, or accompanied by beans and rice. This recipe includes another California favorite, avocado, which perfectly offsets the spicy salsa.

INGREDIENTS
2 tablespoons vegetable oil
4 (5-inch) corn tortillas
1 cup refried beans
    with green chilies
2 tablespoons butter
4 eggs
1 cup shredded
    sharp cheddar cheese
8 slices bacon,
    cooked and crumbled
1 cup salsa
1 avocado, sliced

1. Heat oil in a small skillet over medium-high heat. Fry tortillas one at a time, for a few minutes on each side until firm, but not crisp. Place on paper towels to drain any excess grease.

2. Meanwhile, combine the refried beans and 1 tablespoon of butter in a small saucepan or microwave-safe dish. Cover, and cook until heated through.

3. Heat remaining butter in a skillet and fry eggs to desired consistency.

4. Place fried tortillas onto serving plates. Spread a layer of beans on them. Top with a fried egg, cheese, crumbled bacon, salsa, and sliced avocado.

5. If you prefer your cheese a bit more melted, place under a broiler on high for 45 seconds to 1 minute, or until cheese is hot and bubbling. Serve.

BREAKFAST BURRITOS

SERVES 4

INGREDIENTS
8 eggs
Salt and pepper to taste
4 flour tortillas
1 tablespoon butter
1/2 cup shredded cheddar
*   or Monterey Jack cheese*
1 avocado, diced
1/4 cup scallions, diced
*   (optional)*
4 strips bacon,
*   fried and crumbled*
Red or green salsa

1. Preheat the oven to 250 degrees.

2. In a small bowl, beat the eggs with a fork until blended. Add a dash of salt and pepper if desired. Meanwhile, warm the tortillas on the middle rack of the oven.

3. Melt the butter in a skillet over medium heat.

4. Pour the eggs into the skillet and cook for 1 to 2 minutes. Gently stir with a spatula to let the uncooked egg settle at the bottom of the pan. Cook for another minute or until the eggs are done to your liking.

5. Remove the tortillas from the oven and put them onto plates. Divide the eggs evenly and spoon onto an outer third of each tortilla.

6. Add even amounts of cheese, avocado, scallions, bacon, and salsa on top of the eggs.

7. To roll into burritos, fold in each tortilla at the sides, then roll the tortilla edge with the mixture toward the other edge. Serve immediately.

KITCHEN SINK FRITTATAS

SERVES 4

The name of this classic Italian egg recipe refers to the fact that you can throw pretty much anything into it, and it will be delicious. It's the perfect way to use up the bits and pieces of last night's supper, and one of our favorite uses for left-over spaghetti.

INGREDIENTS
6 eggs
Salt and pepper
2 cups leftover cooked vegetables, meat, pasta, rice, cheese, or whatever you have on hand
1 ½ tablespoons butter

1. Preheat the oven broiler.

2. Whisk the eggs in a large bowl. Season with salt and pepper to taste.

3. Mix in all the other ingredients except the butter.

4. In a large ovenproof skillet (a 9-inch cast-iron frying pan, for example), melt the butter over medium heat.

5. Add the egg mixture and cook until the bottom and edges are set, but the eggs are still runny on top.

6. Remove the skillet from the stovetop and place it under the broiler. Broil for about 3 minutes, until the eggs are set and the top is slightly browned.

7. Let the frittata cool, then cut it into wedges and serve directly from the pan.

Variations:
- **Western:** ham, cheese, peppers, green onions
- **Greek:** feta cheese, olives, plum tomatoes, spinach
- **Southwestern:** salsa, avocado, corn, Monterey Jack cheese, jalapeños, cilantro
- **Italian:** sausage, tomatoes, garlic, basil, Parmesan cheese
- **Veggie:** zucchini, tomatoes, mozzarella, broccoli, mushrooms.

SAVORY BREAKFAST BREAD PUDDING

SERVES 6 TO 8

Use whatever type of bread you have on hand for this recipe. We prefer a *challah* ("egg" bread) or country-style loaf, but if sliced white bread from the supermarket is all you have, this recipe will still work. This dish is perfect breakfast fare when you have a houseful of overnight guests. The pudding is assembled the night before and refrigerated until morning. Leave instructions for the early risers in the crowd to preheat the oven to 350 degrees.

INGREDIENTS

2 tablespoons butter, divided
12 to 16 slices bread
1 1/2 cups shredded cheese (cheddar, Fontina, Swiss, or, preferably, a mixture)
1/2 cup grated Parmesan or Romano cheese
A few tablespoons chopped fresh, tender herbs: parsley, chives, tarragon, basil (optional)
2 1/2 cups whole milk
5 large eggs
1 teaspoon salt
1/4 teaspoon cayenne pepper

1. Butter a 2 1/2-quart soufflé mold, an 8 1/2- by 11-inch pan, or your favorite gratin dish with 1 tablespoon of the butter.

2. Place a layer of bread slices in the dish. If you think the dish you have chosen will accommodate 2 layers of bread, divide the cheeses and optional herbs into halves. If you think it will accommodate 3 layers, divide them into thirds. Sprinkle the first layer of bread with the cheeses and herbs, if you wish, and repeat until you have run out of bread and cheese.

3. In a medium bowl, whisk together the milk, eggs, salt, and cayenne pepper, and pour this mixture over the bread in the baking dish. Dot with the remaining tablespoon of butter. To ensure that the bread is soaked through with the egg mixture, cover with plastic wrap or foil and weigh it down with a plate.

SAVORY BREAKFAST BREAD PUDDING

4. In the morning, preheat the oven to 350 degrees. Place the bread pudding in the oven and bake until golden and set, about 35 to 45 minutes, depending on the size of the pan and the reliability of the oven. A knife inserted into the center of the pudding will come out clean when it is done. Let cool about 10 minutes before serving.

HOME FRIES

SERVES 1

This is a great "leftovers" dish to plan for in advance when you're cooking dinner. But even if you don't have any precooked potatoes to use, they're easy enough to make from scratch. Any kind of potato will be just fine, but we especially like the small red ones. You can serve these with eggs for breakfast; they're also delicious as a side dish for dinner.

INGREDIENTS
2 pounds small red potatoes
Salt and pepper
4 tablespoons vegetable oil
1 small to medium yellow
 onion, peeled and sliced

1. (Eliminate this step if you have leftover cooked potatoes.) Wash the potatoes. If they are larger than 1 1/2 inches in diameter, cut them in half, or to a uniform size. Cover with water in a saucepan and bring to a boil. Then lower the heat and simmer, uncovered, until the potatoes are soft but not fully cooked, about 15 minutes total. Drain and cool.

2. When the potatoes are cool, slice them about 1/4 inch thick. Sprinkle with salt and pepper to taste.

3. Heat the oil in a large frying pan until hot. Add the potatoes and begin frying on one side, over medium-high heat. After several minutes, add the onion. When the bottom side is golden brown, turn and fry the other side, about 10 to 12 minutes total. The potatoes should be crisp outside and soft inside.

4. Remove from the pan with a slotted spoon and drain on paper towels, then serve.

! **Variation:** You can substitute 1/2 cup scallions for the onions. Use only the white, yellow, and light green parts, sliced into rounds. Add to the frying pan as above.

HEAVENLY HASH BROWNS

SERVES 4

The bacon we can take or leave, but there's nothing better with eggs in the morning than hash browns. Need we say more?

INGREDIENTS
2 large baking potatoes
2 tablespoons butter
Salt and pepper to taste

1. Scrub the potatoes and grate them with their skins.

2. Melt the butter in a large skillet over medium-high heat.

3. Add the potatoes to the skillet, spreading them evenly and patting them down with a spatula. Sprinkle salt and pepper on top.

4. Fry the potatoes until they're brown and crispy on the bottom, 5 to 8 minutes.

5. Flip the potatoes, in sections if necessary. Fry for another 5 minutes, or until brown and crispy. Serve hot with ketchup or salsa.

HEARTY
CORNED BEEF HASH

SERVES 4

INGREDIENTS
1 onion, diced
3 tablespoons butter, divided
2 to 3 cups diced
*   cooked potatoes*
1 pound cooked corned beef,
*   finely chopped*
Salt and pepper to taste
A few dashes of Tabasco
4 eggs
1 pound cooked corned beef,
*   finely chopped*

1. In a large frying pan, cook the onion in 2 tablespoons of butter until soft and translucent.

2. Add the potatoes and corned beef and combine well. Add a little water to keep the mixture from sticking to the pan, and bring to a simmer over low heat. Add salt, pepper and Tabasco to taste.

3. While the hash is simmering, heat the remaining butter in a separate frying pan. Add the eggs and cook sunny-side up.

4. Serve the corned-beef mixture on a platter and top with the eggs.

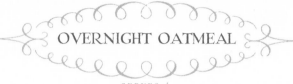

OVERNIGHT OATMEAL

SERVES 4

While many people like their oats rolled, we prefer them "steel-cut." The texture and flavor is much more interesting. The only drawback is that this type of oatmeal takes quite a bit longer to cook, up to 40 minutes. But you can get around this by starting the night before. We love our oatmeal with a splash of cream and brown sugar, maple syrup, or honey drizzled over the top.

INGREDIENTS

1 cup steel-cut oats (like McCann's, or buy it in bulk from a health food store)
1 teaspoon salt
1/2 cup golden raisins
1/2 cup chopped pecans
1/2 cup dried cherries or cranberries
1/2 cup cream

1. The night before you plan to eat the oatmeal for breakfast, measure out 4 cups of water into a 2-quart saucepan. Add the oats, salt, dried fruit, and nuts.

2. Bring the oatmeal to a boil. Turn off the heat, cover, and let sit overnight.

3. In the morning, heat the oatmeal and simmer until tender, about 20 minutes. Add cream. If you have oatmeal left over, store it in the refrigerator. This type of oatmeal reheats well the next day.

! **Variation—Glazed Oatmeal:** Put the cooked oatmeal into a shallow soup bowl. Arrange thinly sliced strawberries, kiwi, banana, and blueberries over the top of the oatmeal in a single layer. Sprinkle evenly with superfine sugar (or light brown sugar that has been rubbed through a sieve) and run under a very hot broiler until the top is caramelized. (If you happen to own a kitchen blowtorch, this works even better.)

CLASSIC PANCAKES

SERVES 4 TO 6

Growing up, my friend Megan's dad hosted Pancake Saturday every week, and friends were always welcome. Her dad, Pat, was king of the kitchen that day, and always put on a show for us while he flipped pancakes. He made his famous batter from scratch, and let the kids shout out requests for special ingredients. Try tossing in chocolate chips, sliced apples, blueberries, raspberries, or anything else your stomach desires! NTF

INGREDIENTS
1 1/2 cups unbleached white
   flour (or cornmeal)
1 tablespoon sugar
1/4 tablespoon salt
1 tablespoon baking powder
3 eggs, separated
4 tablespoons melted butter
   (easily done in the
   microwave)
2 cups milk

1. Preheat the oven to 200 degrees and put a plate in to warm.

2. In a large bowl, combine the dry ingredients.

3. In another bowl, beat the egg yolks with the melted butter and milk. Stir into the flour mixture.

4. Beat the egg whites until they form soft peaks, and gently fold them into the batter.

5. Heat a lightly buttered frying pan over medium-high heat.

6. Drop a large spoonful of batter into the pan to create each pancake. If you are adding extras, sprinkle them on now before the batter sets. After bubbles form and start to dry on the surface of each pancake, flip it and brown it on the other side.

7. Keep the pancakes warm in the oven until ready to serve.

8. Serve with your favorite toppings.

BUTTERMILK PANCAKES

SERVES 2

We didn't grow up with buttermilk pancakes, so we couldn't go to the family recipe box for this one. But so many people we know love them, we couldn't leave them out, either. After much searching, we came up with this perfect recipe, adapted from one by Marion Cunningham, who wrote *The Breakfast Book*.

INGREDIENTS
1 cup buttermilk
1 egg, at room temperature
3 tablespoons butter, melted
3/4 cup all-purpose flour
1/2 teaspoon salt
1 teaspoon baking soda

1. Whisk together the buttermilk, egg, and melted butter in a medium mixing bowl.

2. Stir together the flour, salt, and baking soda in a small bowl until these dry ingredients are well blended, then stir them into the buttermilk mixture until just blended. Do not overmix. A few lumps or traces of flour are okay.

3. Heat a large frying pan, skillet, or griddle to medium hot. Nonstick pans are the easiest. When the pan is hot, grease with a light coating of butter.

4. Spoon out about 3 tablespoons of batter per pancake. Immediately spread out the batter with the back of a spoon so the pancake isn't too thick.

5. When a few bubbles break on top, turn the pancake over and cook briefly until the pancake appears to be slightly puffed up. Serve immediately, preferably with real maple syrup.

SILVER DOLLAR PANCAKES

SERVES 4

These are also known as Bridge Creek Heavenly Hots. Cake flour is essential if you want to make them as light as a feather. Remember to use just a bit of batter for each; this recipe should yield about 50 little pancakes.

INGREDIENTS
4 eggs
1/2 teaspoon salt
1/2 teaspoon baking soda
1/4 cup cake flour
2 cups sour cream
3 tablespoons sugar

1. Put all the ingredients into a blender and mix at a low speed for 1 minute. (Alternatively, you can whisk the eggs in a bowl until blended, then add the rest of the ingredients.)

2. Heat a griddle or large frying pan until quite hot. Add a little bit of vegetable oil to coat the surface.

3. Drop small spoonfuls of batter onto the griddle to make as many 2-1/2-inch rounds as fit in the pan. When small bubbles form on the surface, flip each hotcake and cook the other side briefly.

4. Serve hot with jam, maple syrup, honey, or confectioners' sugar.

SWEDISH PANCAKES

MAKES ABOUT 20 PANCAKES/SERVES 4

My Nana made Swedish pancakes for us (my brothers and me) and then she made them for my daughters. They are thinner than American pancakes, more like crepes, and undeniably delicious. It's easier to make them if your frying pan has a good heavy bottom; this evens out the heat. They cook swiftly over a medium-high flame, and you don't want to burn them. If you find them sticking, melt a bit of butter in the pan first. You can serve with lingonberries, as we always did, but you can also use any kind of jam, or shaved chocolate and powdered sugar, or lemon juice and a sprinkle of regular sugar. If you smear apricot jam atop, then a little whipped cream, and roll up the pancakes, they make a pretty perfect dessert, too. LT

INGREDIENTS
1/3 cup sugar
1 1/3 cups all-purpose flour
4 large eggs
plus 2 large egg yolks
2 1/4 cups milk
8 tablespoons (1 stick) butter,
melted (you can do this in
the microwave)
More butter as needed

1. Sift together the sugar and the flour. Beat together the eggs and milk and add to the dry ingredients, then add the melted butter.

2. Let the batter stand for a half hour or so.

3. On a hot griddle or large, heavy frying pan (around 10 inches in diameter), melt a bit of butter. Pour in about 1/4 cup of the batter and spread it around until it forms a big, thin circle. Brown (this will take less than a minute). Turn the pancake over and brown the other side. Remove to a warming plate in the oven.

4. Repeat until you've used up the batter, adding more butter to the pan as needed.

5. Serve immediately.

CRISPY WAFFLES

SERVES 4 TO 6

These are worth digging out the waffle iron, and are truly delicious with a little butter and maple syrup. If you're feeling adventurous, try the banana walnut version!

INGREDIENTS
2 cups flour
1 tablespoon baking powder
2 cups milk
1/3 cup vegetable oil
2 eggs, separated

1. Preheat a waffle iron.

2. In a large bowl, mix the flour and baking powder.

3. Add the milk, oil, and egg yolks. Beat together with hand mixer until smooth.

4. In a separate bowl, whip the egg whites until stiff. Gently fold into the waffle batter.

5. Spoon about 1/3 cup batter onto the waffle grid. Close the waffle iron and bake until golden and crisp, about 2 to 3 minutes.

6. Serve immediately.

Variation–Banana Nut Waffles: Mash one banana and fold it into the batter. Chop 1/2 cup pecans or walnuts and set aside. Pour the batter onto the waffle grid and then sprinkle a few teaspoons of nuts on top. Bake as directed.

Good bread is the most fundamentally satisfying of all foods; and good bread with fresh butter, the greatest of feasts.

James Beard

FRENCH TOAST

SERVES 6

INGREDIENTS
6 eggs
¹/₂ cup milk
Dash of ground cinnamon or
nutmeg, or ¹/₂ teaspoon
vanilla extract (optional)
12 thick slices brioche,
challah, or your favorite
soft (not crusty) bread
4 tablespoons butter

1. Warm a serving platter in a 250-degree oven.

2. In a wide bowl, whisk together the eggs, milk, and optional flavoring.

3. Soak both sides of the bread slices in the egg mixture until completely moistened.

4. Heat a large frying pan over high heat for 20 seconds, then reduce the heat to medium. Add the butter.

5. When the butter stops sizzling, add the pieces of soaked bread. Cook until golden brown, about 3 to 4 minutes on each side.

6. Keep the French toast warm in the oven and serve immediately when all of the slices are done. Serve with applesauce, syrup, or confectioners' sugar and cinnamon.

FRENCH TOAST CASSEROLE

SERVES 2 TO 4

This is perfect for those lazy Sunday mornings when you want to stay in bed with the paper. The prep work is done the night before, so all you have to do is put on your slippers and pop the dish into the oven. You can even go back to bed for 45 minutes while it bakes and rise to the sweet smell of cinnamon wafting through the house.

INGREDIENTS
1/4 cup packed brown sugar
2 tablespoons melted butter
1 teaspoon ground
  cinnamon, divided
1 apple, peeled, cored,
  and sliced
2 tablespoons raisins
One-third of a 1-pound loaf
  of French bread, sliced
2 eggs, beaten
1/2 cup milk
1 teaspoon vanilla extract
1/4 cup chopped pecans

1. Mix together the brown sugar, the melted butter, and 1/4 teaspoon of the cinnamon. Add the apple slices and raisins; stir to coat. Pour into a greased baking dish. Arrange the bread slices in an even layer over the apple-raisin mixture.

2. Whisk together the eggs, milk, vanilla, and remaining cinnamon. Pour over the bread, covering it evenly so that all slices are soaking in the liquid. Top with chopped pecans. Cover with aluminum foil and refrigerate overnight.

3. Preheat the oven to 375 degrees. Remove the dish from the refrigerator while the oven heats. Bake, covered, for 40 minutes. Remove the cover and bake for an additional 5 minutes. Let stand 5 minutes before serving.

CINNAMON TOAST

SERVES 1

Well, we put this in breakfast because it had to go somewhere. But it could just as easily have been in sweets or lunch or dessert, or dinner, if you ask us! This was always the treat of choice in our house, especially during cold season. Our friend, Maren, is from Minnesota, and the milk toast variation comes from her childhood. NTF

INGREDIENTS
2 *pieces warm, buttered toast*
   of your choice
1/2 *tablespoon*
   ground cinnamon
1 1/2 *tablespoons*
   granulated sugar

1. While the bread is toasting, combine the cinnamon and sugar in a small bowl and mix well.

2. Butter the toast and then immediately spoon cinnamon sugar over the melting butter. Serve immediately!

! **Variation–Cinnamon Milk Toast:** Cut the warm cinnamon toast into bite-size pieces and place in a shallow bowl. Pour 1/2 cup warm milk over the toast. Eat with a spoon before the bread becomes too soggy!

DOUGHNUTS

MAKES 2 DOZEN

I grew up eating freshly made doughnuts from a local mom-and-pop grocer named Dreesen's in East Hampton, New York. Dreesen's was one of those beloved neighborhood fixtures that locals prided as their own and visitors sought out on reputation. Their doughnut machine—a huge, messy, greasy monster of a thing—sat on display in their storefront like a Christmas window at Saks. People would stop and watch the rings of dough as they dropped gracefully into a vat of burning hot oil and sizzled ferociously for a few minutes before emerging perfectly browned and crispy. They came in three varieties: plain, cinnamon sugar, and powdered. Their texture was cakey—not air-filled like the chain store varieties—without being heavy, and went down so easily, it was nothing to eat three or four (or five) before even questioning the wisdom of another bite. When Dreesen's finally shut its doors about a year ago, I despaired. But then I rallied, and decided to carry on the torch myself. So I went in search of the perfect doughnut recipe, and after a great deal of trial and error, I finally got it right—well, right enough. There will never be a doughnut that matches the greatness of Dreesen's, but mine, well, they come respectably close. And that's saying a *lot*. KF

DOUGHNUTS

INGREDIENTS
2 cups buttermilk
2 large eggs, lightly beaten
1 cup granulated sugar
5 cups sifted cake flour
2 teaspoons baking soda
1 teaspoon baking powder
1 teaspoon salt
1/2 teaspoon vanilla extract
1/4 teaspoon cinnamon
1/4 cup melted butter
1/4 cup sour cream
2 quarts of canola oil
  (or other flavorless
  vegetable oil) for frying
1 cup confectioner's sugar,
  sifted

1. In a medium bowl, whisk together the buttermilk, eggs, sugar, and vanilla and set aside.

2. In a large bowl, mix together dry ingredients. Make a well in the center and pour in buttermilk mixture. Slowly stir together. Stir in the melted butter or shortening and knead a few times until dough is smooth, moist, and pliable.

3. Roll out dough on a lightly floured surface to approximately 1/4-inch thickness. Cut with a 2-1/2-inch or larger doughnut cutter.

4. Fill a deep pan or pot with three inches of vegetable oil and heat to 370 degrees (you will need a special candy/deep fry thermometer for this). Fry the doughnuts a few at a time on each side for approximately 1 minute or until golden brown. Remove and drain on paper towels.

5. Allow doughnuts to cool completely, then dredge in bowl of sifted confectioners' sugar.

HONEY WHOLE WHEAT MOMMA BREAD

MAKES 4 LOAVES

The three of us have made this bread together for Thanksgiving for more than 20 years. We make enough to freeze, give away, and toast for breakfast (with butter and honey), not to mention using for sandwiches with stuffing, turkey, lingonberries, and gravy the day after Thanksgiving. Yum. I got this recipe from my girlfriend, Pleasant Coggershall, when we were still in high school. LT

INGREDIENTS

3 packages active dry yeast
4 cups lukewarm water,
*   divided*
1 tablespoon sugar
1 1/2 cups (3 sticks)
*   unsalted butter, melted*
3 tablespoons kosher salt
1/2 cup honey
1/3 to 1/2 cup molasses
5 eggs, room temperature
3 pounds (9 cups)
*   whole wheat flour*
2 pounds (6 cups)
*   unbleached white flour*

1. Empty the yeast into 2 cups of the lukewarm water in a large bowl. Add the sugar. Set aside in a warmish place for 15 to 20 minutes, until foamy.

2. Add—in the following order, and mixing as you go—the butter, salt, honey, molasses, eggs, 2 more cups of the warm water. Finally, bit by bit, mix in the whole wheat flour.

3. Add the white flour slowly (reserving about a cup for kneading), still mixing. Let stand for 10 minutes.

4. Transfer the dough to a lightly floured surface and knead for at least 10 to 15 minutes. If the dough is sticky, sprinkle it lightly with white flour as you work.

5. Butter a large bowl. Turn the dough in the butter to coat. Cover loosely with a warm, damp dishtowel and set aside in a warmish place to rise for 1 1/3 to 2 hours. Punch it down and let it rise again for 30 minutes or so.

HONEY WHOLE WHEAT MOMMA BREAD

6. Preheat the oven to 450 degrees. Butter four 9- by 5- by 3-inch loaf pans or two cookie trays.

7. Transfer the dough to a lightly floured surface. Cut into 4 pieces. Knead each piece, shaping it into a loaf. Press the loaves into the prepared pans or put them on one of the trays. Cover again and let rise for 30 minutes.

8. Bake all the loaves together at 450 degrees for 10 minutes. Reduce the heat to 350. Bake until the bread is golden brown, another 20 to 30 minutes. Remove the loaves from the pans and let them cool.

POPOVERS AND STRAWBERRY BUTTER

MAKES 10-12 POPOVERS

These are inspired by the popovers with strawberry butter served at the Popover Cafe on New York's Upper West Side. The popovers are beyond delicious, but you have to serve them right away, warm from the oven, because they won't keep. The strawberry butter can be made the night before.

STRAWBERRY BUTTER

INGREDIENTS
*4 tablespoons unsalted
    butter, softened
2 tablespoons sugar
1/4 cup strawberries, rinsed,
    hulled, and mashed*

1. Cream together the butter and sugar, then add the mashed strawberries and mix until the color is uniform.

2. Spoon the mixture into a small serving dish or butter mold and refrigerate for about 30 minutes, or until firm.

POPOVERS

INGREDIENTS
*2 eggs
1 cup flour, sifted
1 teaspoon salt
1 cup milk
2 tablespoons
    melted butter*

1. Lightly beat the eggs, and then beat in the flour and salt.

2. Stir in the milk and butter, and blend to make a smooth batter.

3. Butter 10 or 12 muffin cups and fill each two-thirds of the way full.

4. Place in a cold oven, then turn on the heat to 425 degrees and bake for 30 to 35 minutes.

5. Serve immediately.

BLUEBERRY CORN MUFFINS

MAKES 10 TO 16 LARGE MUFFINS

Ten years ago we woke up in an adorable little bed-and-breakfast in St. Helena in the Napa Valley to the smell of delicious warm blueberry corn bread. We prefer to make them as muffins, but if you want a loaf instead, just bake at 400 degrees for an extra 10 minutes or so, or until a fork comes out clean.

INGREDIENTS

1 1/2 cups yellow cornmeal
1 1/2 cups sifted white flour
3/4 cup white sugar
4 1/2 teaspoons baking powder
1 teaspoon salt
1 tablespoon unsalted butter, softened
3 eggs
1 1/2 cups milk
1 cup blueberries

1. Preheat the oven to 425 degrees.

2. In a large bowl, combine the dry ingredients. Cut in the butter.

3. In a separate bowl, beat together the eggs, then add the milk. Add this mixture to the dry ingredients and mix well.

4. Stir in the blueberries.

5. Spoon the batter into greased muffin tins or use paper liners. Bake for 15 to 20 minutes, until the tops are golden brown and an inserted fork comes out clean.

BANANA OATMEAL MUFFINS

MAKES 12 MUFFINS

This low-fat, high-fiber muffin is a great alternative to its less healthy white-flour counterparts. The banana and yogurt make them moist and satisfying.

INGREDIENTS
1 cup rolled oats
1 cup whole wheat flour
1/4 cup packed brown sugar
1 teaspoon baking powder
1/2 teaspoon baking soda
1/2 teaspoon ground cinnamon
*1/4 teaspoon ground
   or freshly grated nutmeg*
2 eggs
2 tablespoons vegetable oil
2 ripe bananas, mashed
*1 cup raisins, fresh or frozen
   blueberries, strawberries,
   rasberries, or the like
   (optional)*
1 cup plain yogurt

1. Preheat the oven to 400 degrees.

2. Prepare muffin tins by using paper liners or by greasing them lightly with butter.

3. Grind the oats in a food processor, or crush them in a plastic bag with a rolling pin.

4. Mix the crushed oats together with all the remaining dry ingredients in a large mixing bowl.

5. In another bowl, mix together all the wet ingredients, bananas, and any optional fruit.

6. Fold the wet mixture into the dry until just combined. Do not overmix.

7. Spoon the batter into muffin tins and bake for 20 to 25 minutes.

STREUSEL
COFFEE CAKE

SERVES 12 TO 16

INGREDIENTS

For the topping:
4 tablespoons butter, softened
1/4 cup flour
1/2 teaspoon ground cinnamon
1/4 teaspoon salt
1 cup packed brown sugar

For the cake:
2 cups flour
3/4 cup granulated sugar
1/4 teaspoon ground nutmeg
1/4 teaspoon ground cinnamon
4 teaspoons baking powder
4 tablespoons unsalted butter,
    softened
2 eggs
1 cup milk
1 cup coarsely chopped
    walnuts or pecans

1. Preheat the oven to 350 degrees.

2. Make the topping: Blend all the ingredients together with a fork. Set aside.

3. Make the cake: Sift together the dry ingredients.

4. Add the butter, eggs, and milk. Stir until smooth.

5. Pour the batter into two 8-inch-round pans or one 12- by 18-inch oblong pan, buttered. Cover with the topping. Sprinkle with the nuts. Bake for 30 minutes or until the top of the cake springs back when touched lightly with your finger.

CINNAMON RAISIN
RUSSIAN COFFEE CAKE

SERVES 10 TO 12

This recipe is a little more involved than the Streusel Coffee Cake, but well worth the effort.

INGREDIENTS

For the filling:
3/4 cup packed brown sugar
1 tablespoon ground
   cinnamon
1 tablespoon cocoa powder
2/3 cup golden raisins
1/2 cup chopped walnuts

For the cake:
1 1/2 cups (3 sticks)
   unsalted butter
1 1/2 cups sugar
3 cups flour
1 1/2 teaspoons baking powder
1 1/2 teaspoons baking soda
1/2 teaspoon salt
3 eggs
2 cups sour cream
2 teaspoons vanilla extract
Confectioners' sugar,
   for serving

1. Preheat the oven to 350 degrees.

2. Grease a bundt pan with butter or cooking spray.

3. Combine all the filling ingredients in a small bowl and set aside.

4. In a medium-size bowl, stir together the flour, baking powder, baking soda, and salt. Set aside.

5. Cream the butter and sugar in a standing mixer, with a handheld mixer, or by hand. Scrape down the sides and bottom of the mixing bowl with a spatula, then add the eggs, sour cream, and vanilla. Mix well.

6. Add the dry ingredients to the butter mixture, scrape down the sides of the bowl, and mix well.

7. Spoon a third of the batter, then half of the filling, into the greased bundt pan. Repeat these layers, ending with batter.

8. Bake for 50 to 60 minutes, or until the cake springs back when touched. Let cool completely before removing.

9. Sift confectioners' sugar lightly over the top before serving.

Lunch

Chicken Noodle Soup

SERVES 6

INGREDIENTS

1 whole chicken
(about 4 pounds)
Kosher salt
(about 2 tablespoons)
1 whole onion, peeled
1 whole turnip,
washed but not peeled
1 whole rutabaga, peeled
6 carrots, peeled and sliced
8 stalks celery,
chopped into 3-inch pieces
2 cubes Knorr chicken
bouillon
1 pound mushrooms, sliced
Fresh dill, tough stems
removed, and chopped
(reserve some for garnish)
1 pound extra-thin
dried egg noodles
Salt and pepper to taste

1. Wash the chicken. Remove the giblets and set aside. Discard, cook, or freeze the liver. (It should not be used in soup stock, as it causes the stock to become cloudy.)

2. Place the chicken in a large soup pot over high heat and cover with water. When the water boils, remove the chicken and pour out the water. Rinse the chicken under cold running water again and thoroughly rinse the pot. (This is to clean the chicken thoroughly and also to ensure a clear stock.)

3. Put the chicken and the giblets (not the liver!) back into the pot. Cover with cool water.

4. Add the kosher salt, onion, turnip, rutabaga, carrots, and celery. Bring to a boil, reduce the heat immediately, and simmer for an hour. You will need to skim the foam off the top of the pot several times, so check on the soup as it cooks. (If the stock boils rapidly, instead of simmering, the foam and fat will emulsify and, again, make the stock cloudy instead of clear.)

Chicken Noodle Soup

5. Add the bouillon cubes and cook for another half hour.

6. Remove the chicken, giblets, onion, turnip, and rutabaga from the pot, leaving the carrots and celery behind. If you have time, refrigerate the stock until the fat congeals on the surface and can be removed.

7. When the chicken is cool enough to handle, shred or cut it into bite-size pieces. Discard the skin and bones, giblets, and necks, along with the onion, turnip, and rutabaga.

8. When ready to serve, return the stock to the stove. Add the mushrooms and the dill, and bring to a simmer. Add salt and pepper to taste.

9. Boil the noodles in a separate pot for about 8 minutes or according to package directions. Drain.

10. Put the noodles and reserved dill into bowls and ladle the soup over them. This soup can be served immediately, stored in the fridge overnight, or frozen indefinitely.

Matzo Ball Soup

SERVES 6

This traditional Jewish soup is a cold weather staple, consisting simply of home-made chicken stock, veggies, and plump matzo balls—round dumplings made primarily of matzo meal and eggs.

Chicken Broth

INGREDIENTS

1 whole chicken (3 to 4 pounds), washed and pat-ted dry, giblets and neck reserved, except for the liver, which should be dis-carded, cooked, or frozen; do not add to the stock

Kosher salt and pepper to taste

2 leeks, cleaned thoroughly and chopped

1 stalk celery, including leaves, chopped

4 large carrots, peeled and cut into 1-inch pieces

2 large onions, peeled and quartered

4 whole cloves garlic, peeled

12 whole peppercorns, crushed

1/2 teaspoon dried thyme

1/2 teaspoon dried dill

1 bunch parsley, leaves only, washed and finely chopped

1. Salt the entire chicken, inside and out, with kosher or coarse salt, and let it stand for 30 minutes.

2. Wash the salt from the chicken and place it in a large stockpot along with all the other ingredients except the parsley. Cover with cold water.

3. Bring to a boil over high heat. When at a rolling boil, reduce the heat to a simmer and cook for 1 to 1 1/2 hours, skimming off any foam that collects on the surface.

4. Remove the chicken from the pot. Once it's cool enough to handle, shred the meat. Discard the giblets, skin, and bones.

5. Salt and pepper the stock to taste. Add the chopped parsley.

6. Keep the stock and vegetables warm while you make your matzo balls.

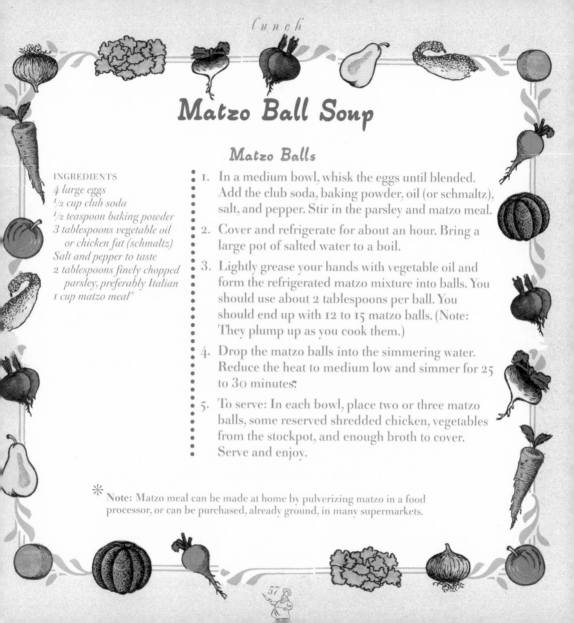

Matzo Ball Soup

Matzo Balls

INGREDIENTS
4 large eggs
¹/₂ cup club soda
¹/₂ teaspoon baking powder
3 tablespoons vegetable oil
or chicken fat (schmaltz)
Salt and pepper to taste
2 tablespoons finely chopped
parsley, preferably Italian
*1 cup matzo meal**

1. In a medium bowl, whisk the eggs until blended. Add the club soda, baking powder, oil (or schmaltz), salt, and pepper. Stir in the parsley and matzo meal.

2. Cover and refrigerate for about an hour. Bring a large pot of salted water to a boil.

3. Lightly grease your hands with vegetable oil and form the refrigerated matzo mixture into balls. You should use about 2 tablespoons per ball. You should end up with 12 to 15 matzo balls. (Note: They plump up as you cook them.)

4. Drop the matzo balls into the simmering water. Reduce the heat to medium low and simmer for 25 to 30 minutes.

5. To serve: In each bowl, place two or three matzo balls, some reserved shredded chicken, vegetables from the stockpot, and enough broth to cover. Serve and enjoy.

* **Note:** Matzo meal can be made at home by pulverizing matzo in a food processor, or can be purchased, already ground, in many supermarkets.

French Onion Soup

SERVES 6

Found on every bistro menu, this traditional French soup is hearty enough to be a meal in itself. If you own oven-proof soup crocks, you can try melting and browning the cheese under the broiler for a couple of minutes in the last step, just before serving.

INGREDIENTS

4 tablespoons butter
6 large Spanish or Vidalia onions, peeled and thinly sliced
4 cloves fresh garlic, peeled and chopped
1/2 teaspoon granulated sugar
1 cup dry white wine
1/2 teaspoon thyme leaves
8 cups (2 quarts) beef or chicken stock, preferably homemade (or canned, low-sodium chicken stock)
Salt and pepper to taste
8 slices French bread, sliced 1/2 inch thick and toasted
Gruyère or Swiss cheese, grated (about 8 ounces)

1. Melt the butter over medium heat in a large frying pan.

2. Add the onions, garlic, and sugar, and stir. Cover the pan, lower the heat, and cook until the onions have softened. This will take about 45 minutes.

3. Uncover the pan and continue to cook, stirring occasionally, until the onions have caramelized.

4. Add the white wine. With a wooden spoon, scrape up the browned bits at the bottom of the pan.

5. Add the thyme and stock, and simmer for 30 minutes. Add salt and pepper to taste.

6. Ladle the soup into bowls. Place two slices of bread on top of the soup in each bowl, sprinkle with cheese, then ladle a bit more soup over the bread to melt the cheese, and serve.

Mushroom-Barley Soup

SERVES 6

This classic winter soup, found in diners and delis across America, is easily made at home. If you don't have homemade beef or chicken stock, including some dried mushrooms adds depth and complexity to this soup. You can usually find inexpensive dried mushrooms in your local supermarket.

INGREDIENTS

1/4 cup dried mushrooms (optional)
1 large onion, peeled and diced
1 large carrot, peeled and diced
1 stalk celery, diced
1 leek, well washed, white and pale green part only, sliced
2 tablespoons butter or oil
1 pound fresh button or cremini mushrooms, sliced
1/2 cup pearl barley
8 cups homemade beef or chicken stock, or 8 cups canned low-sodium chicken broth
Salt and pepper to taste
Chopped fresh parsley or dill (optional)

1. If you're using the dried mushrooms, put them into a small bowl, pour 1 cup boiling water over them, and let them soak for 20 minutes. After soaking, lift the mushrooms out of the water so that you leave the grit behind. Strain the soaking liquid by pouring it into another small container through a sieve lined with a paper towel or coffee filter. Chop the mushrooms, add them to the strained soaking liquid, and set aside.

2. In a 3- to 4-quart pot, sauté the onion, carrot, celery, and leek in the butter or oil until the vegetables are soft, about 10 to 12 minutes.

3. Add the mushrooms, barley, dried mushrooms in their soaking liquid (if using), and stock. Simmer for an hour or until the barley is very tender. Taste for seasoning and adjust. Sprinkle with fresh parsley or dill, if you like, and serve.

Vegetable Soup

SERVES 6 TO 8

This easy soup has virtues well beyond the nutrients it contains. First, you can make it with any combination of vegetables you have on hand (although onions and carrots are essential). Second, it can be made without meat of any kind. Last, it improves as it sits in the refrigerator, should you choose not to eat the whole pot of it on the first day.

INGREDIENTS

2 tablespoons olive or canola oil
2 medium onions, chopped
3 carrots, peeled and diced
1 stalk celery, with leaves, diced
1 leek, washed, white and pale green parts only, sliced
4 cups mixed diced vegetables, such as peeled turnips, potatoes, mushrooms, peppers, zucchini, string beans, corn, sliced cabbage, or tomatoes
1 cup chopped greens, such as spinach, kale, arugula, Swiss chard, or cabbage (optional)
1 (15-ounce) can of chickpeas or cannellini beans, rinsed and drained
8 cups vegetable broth, or chicken or beef stock
1 bay leaf
Salt and pepper to taste
Parmesan cheese (optional)

1. Heat the oil in a large pot over medium heat. Add the onions, carrots, celery, and leek, and sauté until soft, about 10 minutes.

2. Add the 4 cups mixed vegetables, the optional greens and the broth and bay leaf. Simmer for 45 minutes, or until all the vegetables are tender. Add the cooked beans, and simmer for another 20 minutes. If the soup gets too thick, add a bit of water until it reaches the consistency you want. Add salt and pepper to taste and remove the bay leaf.

3. Ladle into deep bowls, grate Parmesan over the top, if you like, and serve.

!

Variations: For additional protein, you can add 1 ½ cups diced chicken, meat, or tofu.

Creamy Tomato Soup

SERVES 6

I grew up on canned tomato soup, which I loved. It was a total treat, especially with buttered toast. But as an adult I wanted a less processed version, and here it is. This is a very filling, rich soup. Add some cooked rice, if you like, or leave the cream out and serve it chilled in the summer. But I love it best as is, on a freezing February afternoon. NTF

INGREDIENTS

1 (28-ounce) can
   diced tomatoes
2 teaspoons sugar
1/4 teaspoon paprika
1/4 teaspoon white pepper
1/2 teaspoon chopped fresh
   basil (or more, to taste)
3 sprigs parsley
1 teaspoon marjoram
1 bay leaf
3 tablespoon butter, divided
1 cup chicken stock
1 chicken bouillon cube
2 tablespoons flour
2 cups half-and-half
1/4 cup sour cream (optional)
Salt to taste
2 tablespoons minced
   parsley, for garnish

1. Combine the tomatoes, sugar, paprika, white pepper, herbs, 1 tablespoon of the butter, the chicken stock, and the bouillon cube in a saucepan. Simmer for about 10 minutes. Discard the bay leaf; transfer the soup to a blender and puree.

2. Melt the remaining 2 tablespoons butter until bubbly. Add the flour, whisk together, and cook over low heat for a minute or two, to cook the flour. Gradually whisk in the half-and-half; cook and stir until smooth and slightly thickened, about 5 minutes.

3. Add the tomato mixture from the blender to the half and half and simmer, stirring occasionally, for 10 minutes.

4. If you're using the sour cream, whisk it into the soup and cook until just heated through; do not boil. Add salt and additional basil to taste. Garnish with minced parsley.

Potato Leek Soup

SERVES 8 TO 10

INGREDIENTS
1 cup diced celery
2 cups diced onions
3 cups sliced leeks, white and
pale green parts only (well
washed and free of grit)
8 tablespoons butter
6 large russet potatoes,
peeled and quartered
2 1/2 quarts (10 cups)
chicken broth
2 cups heavy cream
1/4 cup sour cream
Salt and pepper to taste

1. In a large pot, sauté the celery, onions, and leeks in the butter over medium heat until they are soft.

2. Add the potatoes and chicken broth and bring to a boil. Reduce the heat and simmer until the potatoes are soft. Turn off the heat and let cool.

3. Using an immersion blender, a regular blender, or a food processor, puree until smooth.

4. Put the soup back on the stove and whisk in the heavy cream and sour cream. Bring to a simmer, then remove from the heat.

5. Add salt and pepper to taste and serve.

New England Clam Chowder

SERVES 8

There is another version of clam chowder, made with a tomato base instead of cream, which goes by the name of Manhattan clam chowder. The very notion of such a variation is considered almost a crime in the state of Maine, where they once tried to pass a law against it.

INGREDIENTS

4 tablespoons butter
2 medium yellow onions, peeled and diced
2 tablespoons all-purpose flour
4 cups chicken stock
3 russet potatoes, peeled and diced
4 carrots, peeled and finely diced
1 leek, diced
2 teaspoons fresh thyme leaves
1/4 cup chopped fresh parsley
4 cups chopped cherrystone clams (preferably freshly shucked, but frozen is fine)
2 cups clam juice (reserved from freshly shucked or frozen clams, bottled, or both)
1/2 cup half-and-half or heavy cream

1. Heat the butter in a large, heavy pot and sauté the onions over medium-low heat until translucent, about 10 minutes. Sprinkle the flour over the onions and cook for another few minutes.

2. Add the chicken stock slowly, stirring constantly, making sure that the onion-flour mixture doesn't stick to the bottom of the pot. Add the potatoes, carrots, leek, and herbs. Simmer for another 10 minutes.

3. Add the clams and the clam juice, reduce the heat to low, cover the pot, and slowly simmer until the potatoes are fork-tender (another 15 minutes). Add the half-and-half or cream and cook for another 5 minutes, until heated through. Serve with oyster crackers.

Summer Corn Chowder

SERVES 4

This delicious light and creamy soup is really a dressed-up, healthier version of one of my favorite childhood comfort foods—creamed corn. Best prepared when corn is locally in season and readily available at green markets and farm stands, the key to the soup's success couldn't be simpler: It will be just as sweet and tasty as the corn you use to make it. KF

INGREDIENTS

3 tablespoons butter, divided
2 large leeks, coarsely chopped, white and light green parts only
1 small, sweet Vidalia onion, chopped
1 red pepper, finely diced
4 cups fresh sweet corn kernels, cooked
2 1/2 cups chicken stock
1/2 cup heavy cream (you can substitute whole or skim milk if you prefer)
Salt and pepper

1. In a small frying pan, melt 2 tablespoons of the butter and sauté the leeks and onion until they're soft. Do not brown. Remove from the pan and reserve.

2. Using the same pan, melt the remaining tablespoon of butter and sauté the red pepper until it's also soft and cooked through. Do not brown.

3. Reserve 3/4 cup of the corn and put the rest in a blender or food processor. Add the leeks and onion, along with the chicken stock and heavy cream. Add salt and pepper to taste and blend until finely pureed. If you prefer a thinner consistency, add a little more chicken stock.

4. Pour the soup into a medium saucepan, add the reserved corn kernels, and heat over a medium flame to a simmer. Remove from the heat and spoon the soup into bowls. Sprinkle a bit of diced red pepper in the center of each bowl and serve immediately with a fresh crusty white bread for dipping.

Cream of Chicken Soup

SERVES 8 TO 10

INGREDIENTS

2 cups diced celery
2 cups diced carrots
2 cups diced onions
3 cups sliced leeks, white and
*   pale green parts only,*
*   well-washed and grit-free*
8 tablespoons butter
2 teaspoons fresh mixed
*   herbs, such as rosemary,*
*   thyme, marjoram, and*
*   oregano (or 1 teaspoon*
*   dried mixed herbs),*
*   chopped*
3 bay leaves
1 cup white wine (optional)
2 whole chicken breasts,
*   on the bone, skin removed*
3 quarts (12 cups) home-
*   made chicken stock,*
*   or canned low-sodium*
*   chicken broth*
3 cups heavy cream
Salt and pepper to taste

1. In a large pot, sauté the vegetables in the butter over medium heat until they are soft.

2. Add the herbs and white wine and cook for another 5 to 10 minutes.

3. Add the chicken breasts and the broth, bring to a boil, reduce the heat, and simmer for 20 minutes.

4. Remove the chicken breasts. When they're cool enough to handle, remove the meat from the bones, dice it, and return it to the pot. Discard the bones.

5. Add the cream, bring to a boil, and turn off the heat.

6. If the soup is too thin, try this: Mix together $1/2$ cup all-purpose flour with 4 tablespoons soft butter to form a paste. Tear off a few pieces, roll them into little balls, then whisk them into the soup. Let this simmer until the flour is cooked and the soup thickens. Add as many balls as needed. This thickens the soup without the risk of lumps. (You can use this trick to thicken gravy, too!)

7. Add salt and pepper to taste. This soup can be frozen.

Black Bean and Rice Soup

SERVES 6

INGREDIENTS

1/2 cup chopped onion
1 clove garlic, minced
2 teaspoons vegetable or
    olive oil
1 teaspoon ground cumin,
    or to taste
1 teaspoon chili powder,
    or to taste
4 cups vegetable, chicken, or
    beef broth, or water
2 (15-ounce) cans black
    beans, rinsed and drained
2 cups peeled, seeded,
    and chopped tomatoes
    (fresh or canned)
3/4 cup instant rice or 1 cup
    cooked white or brown rice
1 tablespoon chopped fresh
    oregano, or 1/4 teaspoon
    dried
Salt and pepper to taste
Sour cream or plain yogurt,
    for serving
Picante sauce or prepared
    salsa, for serving

1. Sauté the onion and garlic in the oil until soft. Add the cumin and chili powder and cook until fragrant, about 1 minute.

2. Add the broth, beans, tomatoes, rice, and oregano and cook for 30 to 45 minutes, covered, over low heat.

3. If you would like the soup to have a smoother texture, remove half of it, puree it in a food processor, return it to the pot, and reheat it before serving. Serve with a dollop of sour cream or yogurt, and the salsa.

Split Pea Soup

SERVES 8

This recipe comes from California, where split pea soup is famous. Pea Soup Andersen's of Buellton, California, has built its fortunes on this ubiquitous comfort food. Just remember to stir the soup frequently, running a wooden spoon along the bottom of the pot to make sure that it doesn't burn.

INGREDIENTS

1 tablespoon olive oil
2 medium onions, diced
1/4 pound slab bacon, diced
4 cloves garlic, chopped
1 cup peeled, chopped carrots
1 cup chopped celery leaves
  and stalks
2 cups green
  or yellow dried split peas
1 ham bone
  or smoked ham hock
1 bay leaf and a sprig
  of thyme (optional)
10 cups chicken stock
  or water
Salt and pepper to taste

1. In a large stockpot, heat the olive oil over medium-high heat.

2. Add the onions and bacon and cook until the onions are tender and translucent.

3. Add the garlic and cook for 1 minute. Add the carrots, celery, split peas, ham bone or hock, bay leaf and thyme (if desired), and stock or water.

4. Bring to a boil and simmer over low heat, uncovered, for 1 1/2 to 2 hours, or until the peas have completely softened and turned into a chunky puree. Stir frequently to make sure the soup doesn't stick to the bottom of the pot and burn.

5. Season with salt and pepper and serve immediately, or refrigerate. When reheating, add enough water to prevent scorching.

PEAS
ABOVE
NO
PEAS

Grilled Cheese Sandwich

SERVES 2

It's just bread, cheese, and butter—right? I mean, what could be simpler than a grilled cheese sandwich. And yet this beloved American lunch food seems to have as many preparations as it has devotees. There is first the question of bread: traditionalists may opt for airy white; but wheat, rye, and sourdough are just a few other favorites. Second, there is the type of cheese: classic is, of course, American, but as long as it melts, you can be sure that someone someplace has tried it. And lastly, when it comes to "extras," well, then the list is truly endless: from tomatoes and bacon to pickles and apples, if you can fit it between two slices of bread, you can add it to a grilled cheese sandwich. In our house, my father was the grilled cheese maker. He stuck to the basics: two pieces of thinly-sliced supermarket white bread, two pieces of American cheese, and a generous application of salted butter. The pan was always cast iron and the heat was always medium-low. But my dad had a secret weapon: a heavy solid antique iron which he used to weigh down the sandwich after the first flip. The effect was exquisite. An extremely thin—almost delicate, perfectly browned, crispy on the outside, gooey on the inside, grilled cheese sandwich. Cut immediately into little triangles for little hands, and served alongside one of his famous black-and-white milkshakes, it was an unrivaled after-school snack. And that old iron of his? It sits right next to my stove now, where it is always on hand for when only my dad's grilled cheese will do. Some childhood things are just not meant to be left behind. KF

INGREDIENTS
2 to 3 tablespoons butter, softened
4 slices white bread
4 slices American, Cheddar, Swiss, Fontina or other cheese
Pickles, for serving

1. Butter bread and make two sandwiches with two pieces of cheese per sandwich (butter should be on the outside of the sandwiches).

2. Place in preheated pan with heat on low, and cover the pan. When the cheese starts to melt and the bread has browned, flip each sandwich over and repeat.

3. Serve immediately!

Egg Salad Sandwich

SERVES 2

INGREDIENTS
2 tablespoons mayonnaise
3 hard-boiled eggs (whites
 chopped, yolks mashed)
½ stalk celery, chopped
2 tablespoons chopped onion
Salt and pepper to taste
4 slices of your favorite bread

1. In a large bowl, mix the mayonnaise and egg yolks, then add the egg whites, celery, onion, salt and pepper, and mix well.
2. Serve on bread.

Tuna Salad Sandwich

SERVES 2

INGREDIENTS
1 (6 ounce) can tuna (packed
 in olive oil is the most
 delicious but also the most
 caloric)
4 tablespoons onion,
 finely chopped
2 tablespoon mayonnaise
1 teaspoon lemon juice
Salt and pepper
4 leaves romaine lettuce
4 to 5 slices beefsteak tomato
4 slices of your favorite bread

1. Combine the tuna, onion, mayonnaise, and lemon juice in a bowl.
2. Serve on toasted bread with lettuce and tomato, if desired.

Turkey Club Sandwich

SERVES 2

INGREDIENTS

*6 slices white sandwich
  bread, lightly toasted*
Mayonnaise
*2 leaves romaine or iceberg
  lettuce, washed and dried*
*12 thin slices
  roast turkey breast*
4 thin slices tomato
*6 strips bacon, cut in half,
  cooked until crisp, drained*
8 toothpicks

For each sandwich:

1. Spread three pieces of toast with mayonnaise.

2. Top one piece of toast with a lettuce leaf and two slices of turkey.

3. Cover with a second piece of toast; spread the toast with mayonnaise. On this place a lettuce leaf, two tomato slices, and three strips of bacon.

4. Top with remaining toast slice.

5. Secure with four toothpicks and cut the sandwich into triangle-shaped quarters.

BLT Sandwich

SERVES 2

This sandwich is best if you have fresh tomatoes, which are only astonishingly good in the summer.

INGREDIENTS
4 slices bread
Mayonnaise
4 to 6 slices fresh tomato
8 strips well-cooked bacon
A few romaine or iceberg
lettuce leaves,
washed and dried

For each sandwich:

1. Toast the bread.

2. Spread a generous portion of mayonnaise on a slice of toasted bread.

3. Place two or three slices of tomato on top of the mayo–enough to cover the bread.

4. Add four slices of the bacon, and then the lettuce.

5. Top all with a slice of bread. Cut in half and serve.

Reuben Sandwich

SERVES 2

INGREDIENTS

6 tablespoons sauerkraut,
  drained
4 thin slices corned beef
2 slices Swiss cheese
2 tablespoons
  Thousand Island dressing
4 slices rye bread
Butter

1. Heat the sauerkraut. Thirty seconds in the microwave is enough.

2. Layer the corned beef, cheese, sauerkraut, and dressing between two pieces of rye bread.

3. Heat a skillet over medium heat and use it to melt some butter. Add the sandwich and grill on both sides until the cheese has melted and the bread is golden.

4. Repeat steps 1 through 3 to make second sandwich.

5. Slice sandwiches in half and serve with extra dressing, dill pickles, and coleslaw.

Tuna Melt

SERVES 2

INGREDIENTS

1 (6-ounce) can tuna, drained
2 tablespoons mayonnaise
2 tablespoons butter, divided
4 slices white
  or sourdough bread
2 slices cheddar cheese

1. Mix the tuna and mayonnaise. Heat in the microwave for 40 seconds on high.

2. In a small frying pan over medium heat, melt ½ tablespoon of the butter. Place a slice of bread in the pan with a slice of the cheddar cheese on top. Cover the pan until the cheese melts and the bread is lightly toasted.

3. Put half of the tuna on top of the cheese and another slice of bread on top. Add ½ tablespoon butter, turn, and fry on other side. Remove from the heat.

4. Repeat for the second sandwich.

5. Serve warm.

Sloppy Joe

SERVES 4

Oh, this is so messy and so good. The girls ate it over and over again. Their dad poured it over macaroni. He poured it over rice. He put in on English muffins and he served it on top of toast. We even used it as a sauce for lasagna. For the classic Sloppy Joe, serve on an open hamburger roll, with a knife and fork. LT

INGREDIENTS
2 tablespoons olive oil
2 onions, chopped
4 celery stalks, chopped
4 cloves garlic, chopped
2 pounds lean ground beef
1 cup tomato sauce,
    canned or homemade
3 tablespoons tomato paste
1/2 cup ketchup
1 teaspoon Tabasco sauce
2 teaspoons
    Worcestershire sauce
Salt and pepper to taste
4 hamburger buns

1. Heat the oil in a large, heavy skillet over low heat. Add the onions and celery and cook until soft and lightly browned.

2. Add the garlic and continue cooking for 3 to 4 minutes.

3. Increase the heat to medium high and add the ground beef. Cook for about 10 to 12 minutes, until the meat is browned.

4. Reduce the heat to medium and add the tomato sauce, tomato paste, ketchup, Tabasco, and Worcestershire sauce. Cook, stirring, for about 15 to 30 minutes, until the liquid is reduced and the mixture thickens.

5. Add salt and pepper to taste.

6. Serve on hamburger buns, but be prepared for it to be messy!

The Classic Burger

SERVES 4

Once you've tried this family recipe for our version of the classic American burger, you'll never buy a pre-made pattie again.

INGREDIENTS
1 pound ground turkey or beef
1/2 cup diced onion
1/4 cup ketchup
1/3 cup milk
1/2 cup bread crumbs
1 large egg
1/4 teaspoon salt
1/8 teaspoon pepper
Butter
(for frying-pan method)
4 hamburger rolls

1. Preheat the grill or broiler, or get out the frying pan.

2. In a large bowl, mix the meat, onion, ketchup, milk, bread crumbs, egg, salt, and pepper. Divide and shape into four patties.

3. If you are frying, put a pat of butter into a large frying pan over medium-high heat.

4. Grill, broil, or fry the burgers for about 5 minutes on each side, until the meat is no longer pink in the middle.

5. Serve on rolls with tomato, onion, or lettuce.

Crab Cakes

MAKES 6 CRABCAKES

I came to crab cakes late in life. Thirty-one years of age, to be exact. It took falling for a Baltimorean to fall in love with his hometown dish. And fall I did. Like timber. I quickly learned that Maryland natives take their crab cakes very seriously. And, like New Yorkers when it comes their pizza or bagels, they don't believe a crab cake worth eating can rightly be found outside their home state. My personal introduction was truly authentic. My beau arrived one evening with a parcel containing two softball-sized, perfectly fried, jumbo lump crab cakes, purchased just hours earlier from a Baltimore crab house named Faidley's. I watched as he gently reheated them in a pan with a bit of oil and lovingly plated them with a side of saltines, a few slices of greenmarket tomatoes, and a spoonful of yellow mustard. I can't say if a better crab cake exists—I've never had another kind—but with that first bite, I became a life-long Faidley's loyalist. Faidley's will ship their specialty anywhere in the U.S., but they don't come cheap and it takes a day from order to arrival. So when you just can't wait that long, or can't afford the splurge, I offer you the following home recipe—inspired by the original. KF

INGREDIENTS

*1 pound fresh jumbo
lump crabmeat, drained
(Jumbo lump crabmeat is
sold in cans in the fresh
seafood section of your
market. Check carefully
for stray bits of cartilage
and crabshell before
using by putting it in a
bowl and feeling gently
with your fingers.)*

1. Delicately spread out the crabmeat on a baking sheet, taking care not to break up the lumps. Sprinkle the crumbled saltines evenly over the meat.

2. In a small mixing bowl, stir together the mayonnaise, beaten egg, mustard, Worcestershire, Old Bay Seasoning, and salt. Drizzle over the crabmeat and saltines. Gently use a spoon, or your hands, to fold together all of the ingredients until they're evenly mixed. Let stand for a few minutes.

Crab Cakes

1 cup crushed saltine crackers
  (approximately 20)
1/2 cup mayonnaise
1 large egg, lightly beaten
1 tablespoon Dijon mustard
1 tablespoon
  Worcestershire sauce
1/2 teasoon Old Bay
  Seasoning (optional)
1/4 teaspoon salt
Vegetable oil
Butter

3. Shape into six patties and place on a waxed-paper-covered baking sheet. Cover and refrigerate for an hour.

4. Combine equal parts of vegetable oil and butter in a pan until the mixture is approximately 1/2-inch deep. Heat until very hot. Fry the crab cakes on each side for about 3 minutes, just until brown and crisp on the outside and warmed through. Turn only once, to help keep the crab cakes from breaking up.

5. Drain on paper towels. Serve with tartar sauce, saltines, and a wedge of lemon.

✳ Note: To prepare ahead of time, cook the crab cakes as directed above and refrigerate. Remove the crab cakes from the refrigerator when ready to serve and let them come to room temperature, while preheating the oven to 375 degrees. Place the cakes on a baking sheet and heat in the oven for 8 to 10 minutes, or until they're warmed through.

Fish, to taste right, must swim three times—in water, in butter, and in wine.

Polish proverb

Lobster Rolls

SERVES 4

This quintessential New England sandwich originated in Connecticut. In order to be authentic, it must be served on a toasted, buttered hot-dog bun. Served with a tall glass of lemonade, a lobster roll is the perfect lunch on a hot summer afternoon.

INGREDIENTS

3 to 4 tablespoons
  mayonnaise
1 teaspoon Dijon mustard
2 teaspoons diced scallions
2 tablespoons lemon juice
Salt and pepper to taste
Meat from 2 (1-pound)
  lobsters, cooked, chilled,
  and cut into small chunks
1/2 cup chopped lettuce (we
  like iceberg or romaine)
2 celery ribs, finely chopped
4 buttered hot-dog rolls

1. Mix the mayonnaise, mustard, scallions, lemon juice, salt, and pepper. Then add the lobster meat, chopped lettuce, and celery.

2. Place the open buttered rolls facedown in a hot skillet for about a minute to toast.

3. Fill the hot-dog rolls, and feast.

Chicken Fingers

SERVES 4

Little mouths just love these, but we think they are worthy of adult tastes as well.

INGREDIENTS

*4 boneless,
    skinless chicken breasts
1 large egg
3 tablespoons milk
1/4 cup grated
    Parmesan cheese
1 1/2 cups dry bread crumbs
Salt and pepper to taste
2 tablespoons butter
2 tablespoons canola oil*

1. Slice the chicken breasts into finger-size strips.

2. In a bowl, whisk together the egg, milk, and cheese.

3. In another bowl, mix the bread crumbs, salt, and pepper.

4. Dip the chicken slices in the egg mixture and then roll them in the bread crumbs. Place on waxed paper in a single layer.

5. Melt the butter and oil in a large skillet and cook the chicken fingers over medium-high heat. Do not overcrowd; cook in batches if necessary. Cook for about 15 minutes, turning the chicken strips as they brown. Remove and drain on paper towels.

6. Alternatively, you can bake the strips in the oven at 425 degrees for 25 minutes, turning the pieces over midway.

7. Serve with dips such as honey mustard, blue cheese dressing, or BBQ sauce.

Old-Fashioned Deviled Eggs

MAKES 12

INGREDIENTS
6 hard-boiled eggs
4 tablespoons mayonnaise
1 ½ teaspoons
   Dijon mustard
Salt and pepper to taste
1 tablespoon minced
   fresh parsley
Dash of paprika

1. Remove the eggshells and slice the eggs in half lengthwise.

2. Scoop out the yolks and mash them in a bowl along with the mayonnaise, mustard, salt and pepper, and parsley. With a mini whisk or fork, beat the mixture until it is light and fluffy.

3. Arrange the egg whites on a plate. Spoon equal amounts of the egg yolk mixture into the hollows of the egg whites. Sprinkle the top of each egg with a dash of paprika.

Chowder breathes reassurance.
It steams consolation.

Clementine Paddleford

Scones

MAKES ABOUT 1 DOZEN SCONES

Enjoying teatime is a great excuse for spending a peaceful hour with some friends or a good book. Scones are the traditional accompaniment, and this recipe could not be easier to make. Serve them warm or at room temperature: They need only butter or clotted cream, your favorite preserves, and a pot of freshly brewed tea.

INGREDIENTS
2 cups all-purpose flour
¼ cup sugar
2 teaspoons baking powder
¼ teaspoon salt
6 tablespoons cold butter, diced
½ cup dried currants or raisins
½ cup heavy cream
2 large eggs
2 teaspoons water

1. Preheat the oven to 400 degrees. Use a nonstick baking sheet, or line a regular baking sheet with parchment paper or foil.

2. Sift together the flour, sugar, baking powder, and salt into a large bowl. Add the cold butter. Using your fingertips, rub the flour mixture and butter together until the mixture resembles coarse meal. Stir in the currants or raisins.

3. Whisk together the cream and one of the eggs in a small bowl. Add the egg mixture to the flour mixture; stir just until combined.

4. Gather the dough into a ball and knead lightly. Roll out the dough on a floured surface to ¾-inch thickness. Using a 2-inch round cookie cutter, cut out scones. Gather the scraps, reroll, and cut out additional scones. Place the scones on the prepared baking sheet.

Scones

5. In a small bowl, whisk together the remaining egg and 2 teaspoons of water. Brush this mixture over the tops of the scones. Bake the scones until golden brown, about 20 minutes. Transfer them to a rack and cool slightly before serving.

Banana Bread

MAKES 1 LOAF

If you put your overly ripe bananas in the freezer instead of throwing them away (they will turn black but won't go bad), you will always have the perfect ingredients on hand for this delicious and healthy bread.

INGREDIENTS
*8 tablespoons (1 stick)
  unsalted butter, softened,
  plus 1 tablespoon for
  greasing the pan
2 cups all-purpose flour
1 tablespoon baking powder
1/4 teaspoon salt
1 cup packed brown sugar
1 teaspoon grated
  lemon rind
2 eggs
2 cups mashed bananas
  (about 4 or 5 very ripe
  bananas)
1 cup chopped walnuts
1/4 teaspoon ground
  nutmeg
1/2 teaspoon vanilla extract
1/2 teaspoon ground
  cinnamon*

1. Preheat the oven to 350 degrees. Grease a 9- by 5- by 3-inch pan with 1 tablespoon of the butter.

2. In a large bowl, mix together the flour, baking powder, and salt.

3. In a separate bowl, blend the remaining butter, sugar, and lemon rind until smooth. Beat in the eggs, and then add the flour mixture.

4. Mix in the bananas, walnuts, nutmeg, and vanilla.

5. Pour the batter into the prepared pan and sprinkle with the cinnamon.

6. Bake for 1 hour. Check to see if the sides have pulled away from the pan; if not, bake for another 10 minutes.

7. Let bread cool in pan for ten minutes before removing it.

Zucchini Bread

MAKES 2 LOAVES

I started baking zucchini bread one summer when there was so much zucchini in the garden that it was starting to rot faster than we could eat it. It's easy (much simpler to grate zucchini than to grate carrots, if you haven't tried before) and delicious, even if you don't like zucchini. Have a slice with yogurt for breakfast or a slice with tea as an afternoon snack. Or ice it with the Cream Cheese Icing on page 123 and serve it for dessert! NTF

INGREDIENTS
Butter for greasing the pans
3 cups flour
1 teaspoon salt
1 teaspoon baking soda
3/4 teaspoon baking powder
2 teaspoons ground cinnamon
1/2 teaspoon ground nutmeg
1 cup packed brown sugar
1 cup granulated sugar
1 cup vegetable oil
3 eggs
2 to 2 1/2 cups grated zucchini
2 teaspoons vanilla extract
1 cup chopped nuts
1 cup raisins (optional)

1. Preheat the oven to 325 degrees. Grease two (9- by 5-inch) loaf pans with butter, then coat with flour and set them aside.

2. Combine the flour, salt, baking soda, baking powder, cinnamon, and nutmeg in a medium-size bowl. Set aside.

3. Whisk together the sugars, oil, and eggs in a large mixing bowl. Stir in the zucchini, vanilla, and nuts.

4. Add the dry ingredients. Stir to mix and add the raisins, if desired.

5. Pour into the prepared pans. Bake for about 1 hour, or until the top springs back when touched lightly and an inserted toothpick comes out clean. Let the loaves cool for 10 minutes before you remove them from the pans.

Pound Cake

MAKES 2 LOAVES

We tested a lot of recipes before getting this one right. The original pound cake is so named because it has a pound of sugar, a pound of butter, and a pound of flour. We tried that recipe first. But honestly, this is *much* better.

INGREDIENTS

2 ¼ cups all-purpose flour, plus more for flouring pans
teaspoon salt
1 teaspoon baking powder
2 cups sugar
1 cup (2 sticks) unsalted butter, softened
5 eggs
¼ cup sour cream
¼ cup milk
2 teaspoons vanilla extract

1. Preheat the oven to 350 degrees. Grease and lightly flour two (9- by 5-inch) loaf pans and set them aside.

2. Combine the flour, salt, and baking powder in a small bowl and set aside.

3. Using an electric mixer, mix the sugar and butter together in large bowl until creamy. Beat in the eggs one at a time. Scrape the bottom and sides of the mixing bowl with a rubber spatula.

4. Add the sour cream, milk, and vanilla. Mix well.

5. Add the flour mixture in two parts, and beat just until blended.

6. Divide the batter between the loaf pans and bake for 50 to 55 minutes, or until they're golden brown and a toothpick comes out clean when inserted.

7. Let the cakes cool for 10 minutes before removing them from the pans.

Cranberry Walnut Bread

MAKES 2 LOAVES

INGREDIENTS

4 cups all-purpose flour
1 tablespoon baking powder
1 teaspoon baking soda
3/4 teaspoon ground cinnamon
8 tablespoons (1 stick) unsalted butter, melted
1 1/3 cups packed brown sugar
1/2 cup granulated sugar
1 tablespoon grated orange rind
1 1/2 cups orange juice
2 eggs
2 cups fresh cranberries, chopped
1 cup dried cranberries, chopped
1 cup walnuts, chopped

1. Preheat the oven to 350 degrees. Butter and flour two loaf pans, each 9- by 5-inches.

2. In a medium bowl, combine the flour, baking powder, baking soda, and cinnamon. In a separate bowl, combine the melted butter, sugars, orange rind, orange juice, and eggs. Blend the flour mixture into the sugar-orange mixture. Stir in the cranberries and nuts.

3. Divide the batter evenly between the pans. Bake for 55 to 60 minutes or until a toothpick inserted into the center comes out clean.

4. Cool the loaves in the pans for at least 10 minutes before unmolding.

Gingerbread

SERVES 8

This gingerbread improves in flavor over the course of several days. It even tastes great when it has gone a bit dry—just pop a slice in the toaster, add some butter, and serve with a cup of tea. Buttermilk is now available powdered in the baking section, so you don't need to buy an entire fresh quart just to make this cake.

INGREDIENTS

*8 tablespoons
(1 stick) unsalted butter*
*1/2 cup packed light or
dark brown sugar*
1/2 cup molasses
2 eggs
1 1/2 cups all-purpose flour
1/2 teaspoon baking soda
*1 generous tablespoon
ground ginger*
*1 teaspoon
ground cinnamon*
1/4 teaspoon ground cloves
*1/4 teaspoon ground
allspice*
1/2 cup buttermilk
1/2 cup dried zante currants

1. Preheat the oven to 350 degrees. Butter an 8- or 9-inch round cake pan.

2. Cream the butter with the brown sugar, beating until fluffy. Add the molasses and mix well.

3. Beat in the eggs.

4. In a separate bowl, mix together the flour, baking soda, ginger, cinnamon, cloves, and allspice. Stir the flour mixture into the egg mixture.

5. Add the buttermilk and blend. Stir in the currants. Pour the batter into the buttered cake pan and bake for 20 to 30 minutes, or until a toothpick inserted in the middle comes out clean.

Classic Sugar Cookies

MAKES 2 ¹/₂ DOZEN COOKIES

INGREDIENTS
¹/₂ cup (1 stick) butter,
room temperature
¹/₂ teaspoon salt
1 teaspoon grated
lemon rind
1 ¹/₄ cups sugar, divided
2 eggs
2 tablespoons milk
2 cups flour
1 teaspoon baking powder
¹/₂ teaspoon baking soda

1. Preheat the oven to 400 degrees.

2. In a large mixing bowl, cream together the butter, salt, lemon rind, and 1 cup of the sugar.

3. Add the eggs and milk. Using a rubber spatula, scrape the bottom and sides of the bowl. Mix well.

4. In a separate bowl, combine the flour, baking powder, and baking soda, and gradually add to the above mixture. Mix well.

5. Drop the mixture onto a greased cookie sheet 1 rounded tablespoon at a time, 2 inches apart.

6. Place remaining ¹/₄ cup sugar in a small bowl. Butter the bottom of a glass, dip it into the sugar, and flatten a cookie. Repeat until all of the cookies are flattened.

7. Bake for 8 to 10 minutes until light golden. Transfer the cookies to wire racks and let them cool.

Cookies are made of
butter and love.

Norwegian proverb

Chocolate Chip Cookies

MAKES ABOUT 96 COOKIES

Have you ever noticed how everyone is always trying to outdo everyone else when it comes to chocolate chip cookies? Well, try these. They are crispy, delicious, and especially great served warm. If you want them more chewy and less crispy, remove one egg. LT

INGREDIENTS
4 ½ cups unbleached all-purpose flour
2 teaspoons baking soda
½ teaspoon salt
1 ½ cup brown sugar
1 ½ cup granulated white sugar
2 cups (4 sticks) butter, softened
2 cups chopped walnuts
4 cups (24 ounces) semi-sweet chocolate chips
5 eggs, slightly beaten
2 teaspoons vanilla extract

1. Preheat oven to 375 degrees.

2. Combine flour, baking soda, salt, and sugars and mix well.

3. Using your fingers, mix in the butter until it is crumbly.

4. Add nuts and chocolate chips. (You can stop here if you like and store dough for up to six months in the freezer.)

5. Beat eggs and vanilla together, then add to the cookie mixture with your fingers and blend.

6. Using a tablespoon, drop small mounds (you should be able to have 16 cookies on a sheet at a time) onto an ungreased or parchment covered cookie sheet.

7. Bake for 10 to 12 minutes or until brown. Remove from hot sheet immediately.

Oatmeal Cookies

MAKES ABOUT 4 DOZEN COOKIES, DEPENDING ON SIZE

Crunchy on the edges, soft in the middle, these are fast, easy, and always a hit!

INGREDIENTS
2 cups all-purpose flour
1 teaspoon baking soda
1 teaspoon ground
cinnamon
½ teaspoon salt
1 cup (2 sticks) unsalted
butter, softened
1 cup firmly packed
brown sugar
½ cup granulated sugar
2 eggs
1 tablespoon vanilla extract
2 cups uncooked rolled oats
½ cup raisins (optional)

1. Preheat the oven to 350 degrees.

2. In a small bowl, combine the flour, baking soda, cinnamon, and salt. Set aside.

3. Using an electric mixer, beat together the butter and sugars in a large bowl until creamy. Add the eggs and vanilla and mix well. Scrape the bottom and sides of the bowl with a rubber spatula.

4. Stir in the flour mixture, oats, and raisins (if desired), mixing well.

5. Using a tablespoon, measure out the dough onto a greased baking sheet in spoonfuls about 1 1/2 inches apart. Bake for 10 to 15 minutes, until lightly golden for chewy oatmeal cookies, or more browned if you prefer them crispy.

6. Cool the cookies for about a minute on the baking sheet before removing with a flat spatula.

Peanut Butter Cookies

MAKES ABOUT 2 ½ DOZEN COOKIES.

If I never baked another sweet, my husband would be happy eating these alone for the rest of his life. If you love peanut butter, as he does, and have a sweet tooth, then this is the cookie for you, too. NTF

INGREDIENTS
½ cup honey
*½ cup crunchy
    peanut butter*
*4 tablespoons (½ stick)
    unsalted butter, softened*
1 egg
1 cup all-purpose flour
¼ teaspoon baking powder
Pinch of salt

1. Preheat the oven to 375 degrees. Grease a cookie sheet or lay a sheet of parchment on it.

2. Put the honey, peanut butter, butter, and egg into a mixing bowl and beat with an electric mixer for 2 minutes (or just beat well by hand).

3. In a separate bowl, combine the flour, baking powder, and salt. Gradually add this to the peanut butter mixture. Mix well.

4. Drop the mixture onto the cookie sheet, 1 tablespoon at a time, around 2 inches apart.

5. Bake for 12 to 15 minutes until lightly browned. Transfer the cookies to wire racks and let them cool.

Molasses Crisps

MAKES 4 DOZEN

This is a great recipe to have in your kid-friendly repertoire—there are plenty of jobs for them to do. Once chilled, the dough is to be rolled into walnut-size balls, then the tops are dipped in sugar. After being placed on a cookie sheet, each ball of dough should be sprinkled with a few drops of water to produce the crackled surface. After all the hard work, these crispy, homey cookies are the delicious reward. This recipe is adapted from one found in the first edition of Betty Crocker's *Picture Cookbook*, published in 1950.

INGREDIENTS
3/4 cup Crisco Zero Trans Fat Shortening
1 cup packed brown sugar
1 large egg
1/4 cup molasses
2 1/2 cups all-purpose flour
2 teaspoons baking soda
1/4 teaspoon salt
1/2 teaspoon ground cloves
1 teaspoon ground cinnamon
1 teaspoon ground ginger
1/4 cup granulated sugar, spread out on a small plate

1. Preheat the oven to 375 degrees.

2. Mix together the shortening, brown sugar, egg, and molasses.

3. In another bowl, mix together the flour, baking soda, salt, cloves, cinnamon, and ginger. Stir this into the molasses mixture until well blended. Chill until firm.

4. Roll the dough into balls about the size of large walnuts. Dip their tops in the granulated sugar and place them, sugared-side up, 3 inches apart on a greased baking sheet. Flatten each cookie using the bottom of a glass.

5. Sprinkle each cookie with a few drops of water to produce a crackled surface.

6. Bake for 10 to 12 minutes, until set but not hard. The cookies will become firmer as they cool.

Swedish Gingerbread Cookies

YIELDS 15 TO 30 DOZEN COOKIES, DEPENDING ON SIZE AND THICKNESS

Swedish gingerbread cookies are classic Christmas fare in Scandinavia. Traditionally, they are very thin and crispy. The decorating is the best part— family and friends (and many children) can spend hours over a single tray! You'll need a collection of cookie cutters. But if you start with a star, a heart, a moon, a man, a woman, and a Christmas tree, you are good to go.

INGREDIENTS

7 cups all-purpose flour
1 tablespoon baking soda
1 tablespoon
ground cinnamon
1 tablespoon ground cloves
1 tablespoon ground ginger
2 cups sugar
1/2 cup (1 stick) unsalted
butter, room temperature
1/2 cup bacon fat, room
temperature, or another
1/2 cup butter
1 cup dark (or light)
corn syrup
1 1/4 cups heavy cream

1. In a bowl, mix together the flour, baking soda, and spices.

2. Beat the sugar, butter, and bacon fat together in a separate bowl. Stir in the corn syrup and heavy cream. Slowly add the dry ingredients and blend well.

3. Flour your hands and toss the dough quickly on a floured surface. Roll into a ball, then divide that into three balls. Cover each in waxed paper. Put them in the refrigerator to chill for at least 2 hours.

4. Preheat the oven to 375 degrees. Line baking sheets with parchment paper.

5. Turn out the dough onto a lightly floured surface, 1 ball at a time, and roll out. You can roll the dough pretty thin for crisp cookies. You can also roll the dough directly onto waxed paper.

Swedish Gingerbread Cookies

6. Cut with cookie cutters. Use a spatula to move the shapes onto the cookie sheets. You can decorate the cookies with colored sprinkles or sugar crystals before baking, but do not ice.

7. Bake for approximately 12 minutes. (If you have made your cookies thicker, lower the oven temperature to 350 degrees and bake slightly longer, for 15 to 20 minutes.) When the cookies are beginning to brown, remove them from the oven and slide the parchment off the baking sheet. When the cookies have cooled a bit, slide them off the parchment. Cool the cookie sheet before using it again. If you have baked the cookies without decorations, wait until they are completely cool before icing.

! **Variations—Christmas Tree Ornaments:** If you want the cookies to serve as ornaments, form a hole in each with a plastic straw or a wooden or metal skewer before baking. For this purpose, you can make the cookies thicker and bake them longer at a lower temperature (approximately 25 to 30 minutes at 300 to 325 degrees).

Scottish Shortbread

MAKES ABOUT 1 DOZEN SCONES.

INGREDIENTS

*2 sticks (1 cup) unsalted
   butter, softened to room
   temperature
1/2 cup confectioners' sugar
2 cups all-purpose flour,
   sifted
1/4 teaspoon salt*

1. Preheat the oven to 325 degrees.

2. In a medium-size bowl, cream together the butter and sugar with an electric mixer.

3. Blend the flour and salt into the butter mixture by hand until thoroughly mixed.

4. Press the dough into an ungreased 9- by 9-inch baking pan. Pierce the dough with a fork every 1/2 inch.

5. Bake the shortbread until it's firm when lightly pressed in the center, about 25 to 30 minutes. (Shortbread should not be brown.) Cut into squares while still warm so pieces won't break. Arrange them on a serving dish and serve with homemade jam (see the recipes at the end of this chapter).

Lemon Squares

MAKES ABOUT 36 SQUARES

INGREDIENTS
For the crust:
3 ½ cups all-purpose flour
¼ cup confectioners' sugar
¼ teaspoon salt
1 ¾ cups (3 ½ sticks)
    unsalted butter,
    cut into bits

For the filling:
6 large eggs
3 cups granulated sugar
2 tablespoons grated
    lemon zest
¾ cup freshly squeezed
    lemon juice
⅔ cup all-purpose flour
1 teaspoon baking powder
Confectioners' sugar,
    for dusting

1. Preheat the oven to 350 degrees.

2. Make the crust: In a large bowl, sift together the flour, sugar, and salt. With a pastry blender or two knives, cut the butter into the flour mixture until it has the consistency of cornmeal.

3. Press the dough into a jelly roll pan (10- by 15-inches, with 2-inch-high sides).

4. Bake for 20 minutes, and then let it cool.

5. While the crust is baking, prepare the filling: Beat the eggs until blended, then beat in the remaining ingredients (except the confectioners' sugar) slowly, in the order listed. Blend until smooth.

6. Pour the mixture over the cooled crust and bake for 25 more minutes.

7. Set the pan on a rack to cool. Use a sharp knife to carefully cut into 2-inch squares. Dust with confectioners' sugar before serving.

Pumpkin Bars with Cream Cheese Icing

MAKES APPROXIMATELY 2 DOZEN BARS

Pumpkin Bars

INGREDIENTS
4 eggs
1 ²/3 cups sugar
1 cup applesauce,
  unsweetened
1 (15-ounce) can unsweet-
  ened pumpkin puree
2 cups all-purpose flour
2 teaspoons baking powder
1 teaspoon baking soda
2 teaspoons
  ground cinnamon
1 teaspoon salt

1. Preheat the oven to 350 degrees.

2. Whisk together the eggs, sugar, applesauce, and pumpkin puree.

3. In a separate bowl, mix together the flour, baking powder, baking soda, cinnamon, and salt. Combine the wet and dry ingredients.

4. Spread the batter into a greased 13- by 9- by 2-inch baking pan and bake for 25 to 30 minutes, or until the top of the cake springs back when touched lightly with a fingertip and a toothpick comes out clean when inserted. Cool.

Cream Cheese Icing

INGREDIENTS
1 (8-ounce) package cream
  cheese
8 tablespoons (1 stick)
  unsalted butter, softened
2 cups confectioners' sugar
1 teaspoon vanilla extract

With an electric mixer, cream the cream cheese and butter, then add the sugar and vanilla. Spread over the cooled Pumpkin Bars and cut into squares.

PB & J Bars

MAKES 8 BARS

A snackable (and portable) version of a classic pairing.

INGREDIENTS
2 cups uncooked rolled oats
1/3 cup peanut butter
1/2 cup grape jelly

1. Preheat the oven to 350 degrees.

2. In a medium bowl, combine all of the ingredients and mix thoroughly.

3. Spread the mixture into greased 9- by 11-inch square baking pan.

4. Bake for 25 minutes. Let cool.

5. Cut into bars. These can be wrapped individually.

Marshmallow Rice Treats

MAKES ABOUT 2 DOZEN TREATS

So why would we include a treat that you can easily find the recipe for on the side of a cereal box? Because, our version is better! Slightly modified from the original over many years and many batches, this recipe produces a chewier, more buttery version that I swear will make people ask you why yours always seem to turn out so much better than theirs. And when they do, I recommend you smile innocently and reply, "I just follow that same old recipe on the side of the box…" KF

INGREDIENTS
40 regular marshmallows*
3 tablespoons unsalted
*   butter*
1 teaspoon vanilla extract
5 cups toasted rice cereal
*   (like Rice Krispies*)*

*approximately 1 (10-ounce)
*   bag*

1. Measure cereal into a large heat-resistant mixing bowl. Set aside.

2. Melt marshmallows and butter in double boiler. Add vanilla and stir until smooth.

3. Pour melted marshmallow mixture into the bowl of cereal and stir until evenly coated.

4. Press into a 9- by 11-inch baking pan lined with wax paper.

5. When the treats are cool, cut into 2-inch squares and store in a sealed container.

Snickerdoodles

MAKES ABOUT 4 DOZEN COOKIES

We have no idea where this cinnamon sugar cookie got its name—but there's definitely no Snickers in a snickerdoodle!

INGREDIENTS

1 cup (2 sticks) unsalted butter, softened to room temperature
1 1/2 cups plus 2 tablespoons sugar, divided
2 eggs, room temperature
1 teaspoon vanilla extract
2 3/4 cups all-purpose flour
2 teaspoons cream of tartar
1 teaspoon baking powder
2 tablespoons ground cinnamon

1. In a large mixing bowl, cream together the butter, 1 1/2 cups of the sugar, the eggs, and the vanilla.

2. Sift together the flour, cream of tartar, and baking soda. Stir into the creamed mixture. Chill the dough in the refrigerator for 1 hour.

3. Preheat the oven to 400 degrees.

4. Roll the dough into walnut-size balls. Combine the remaining sugar and the cinnamon in a shallow dish. Roll the dough balls in this mixture until well coated.

5. Place the cookies about 2 inches apart on an ungreased cookie sheet. Bake for 8 to 10 minutes until light brown, but still soft.

Meringues

MAKES 1 CAKE, 6 BOWLS, OR 20 MERINGUES

INGREDIENTS
4 egg whites (1/2 cup)
1/2 teaspoon cream of tartar
3/4 cup granulated sugar
3/4 cup confectioners' sugar

1. Preheat the oven to 200 degrees.

2. In a scrupulously clean (grease-free) mixing bowl, beat the egg whites until very frothy. Add the cream of tartar and beat at medium speed while slowly adding the sugar. Beat at high speed until very stiff peaks form when you lift the beater slowly.

3. For meringue cookies, drop the mixture by tablespoons onto a baking sheet lined with parchment paper or directly onto a Teflon baking sheet or glass baking dish. Do not butter or flour the surface. Bake for 2 to 2 1/2 hours. Do not let these brown. If your oven has a pilot light, a better method is to make the meringues the night before: Bake 1 hour at 200 degrees, then turn off the oven and leave them in the oven until morning. They will be perfect.

Variations:
- Line a second baking sheet with parchment. Divide the meringue mixture in half and form one 8-inch round disk of meringue on each baking sheet. Bake as directed. When cool, layer strawberries and whipped cream between the two disks, top with more, and serve.
- Form the meringue into six small "bowls": Place six mounds of meringue on the baking sheet. Use the back of a tablespoon to make a deep hollow in each mound. Bake as directed. When cooled, fill bowls with ice cream and chocolate sauce, sliced peaches with raspberry sauce, chocolate mousse and whipped cream (see pages 330, 256), or fresh berries.

Pudge Brownies

MAKES 2 DOZEN BROWNIES

Nothing is better than the smell of freshly baked brownies. And these are the best brownies ever. As much fudge as brownie, this simple recipe will become a staple for you, too.

INGREDIENTS
2 cups (4 sticks; 1 pound) unsalted butter
1 pound semisweet chocolate
6 extra-large eggs, beaten
2 tablespoons vanilla extract
2 1/2 cups sugar
1 1/2 cups all-purpose flour
1 tablespoon baking powder
1 teaspoon salt
1 cup chocolate chips

1. Preheat the oven to 325 degrees. Grease two 13- by 9- by 2-inch baking pans.

2. Melt together the butter and semisweet chocolate in a double boiler over simmering water. Let this mixture cool slightly (do not let it harden). Then stir in the eggs, vanilla, and sugar.

3. Sift together the flour, baking powder, and salt, and stir into the chocolate mixture. Stir in the chocolate chips.

4. Spread the batter evenly in the prepared pans. Bake for approximately 35 to 40 minutes. Do not overbake—a toothpick will not come out clean when inserted! The center should no longer jiggle, being just slightly set. As the brownies cool, they will firm up and become like brownie "fudge." Cool completely before cutting and serving.

What are memories made of?
Of family, and of dinners, and of tastes.

Jacques Pepin

Mississippi Mud Bars

MAKES 18 TO 24 BARS

INGREDIENTS

*1/2 cup (1 stick) unsalted
butter, softened to room
temperature*
3/4 cup packed brown sugar
1 teaspoon vanilla extract
1 egg, room temperature
1 1/3 cups all-purpose flour
1/2 teaspoon baking soda
1/4 teaspoon salt
1/2 cup chopped pecans
*1 cup chocolate chips,
divided*
*1 cup white chocolate chips,
divided*

1. Preheat the oven to 375 degrees.

2. In a large bowl, cream together the butter, sugar, and vanilla. Beat in the egg until the mixture is light and creamy.

3. Mix in the flour, baking soda, and salt until blended. Fold in the nuts, 3/4 cup of the chocolate chips, and 3/4 cup of the white chips.

4. Spread the cookie dough mixture evenly into a greased 13- by 9- by 2-inch baking pan. Bake for 23 to 28 minutes, or until golden brown on top and the center feels firm. Remove from the oven and immediately sprinkle the remaining chocolate and white chips on top, letting them melt.

5. Spread the melted chips into swirls with a butter knife across the top of the pan cookie. Let the cookie cool before cutting into bars.

Chocolate Fudge

MAKES ABOUT 100 SQUARES

INGREDIENTS

*2 ³/4 cups (18 ounces)
semisweet chocolate
chips
4 cups (8 ounces; 1/2 bag)
miniature marshmallows
1 cup (2 sticks) unsalted
butter, melted
1 tablespoon vanilla extract
2 cups chopped walnuts
(optional)
1 (12-ounce) can
evaporated milk
4 ¹/2 cups sugar*

1. Butter a 13- by 9- by 2-inch baking pan. Set aside.

2. In a large mixing bowl, combine the chocolate, marshmallows, butter, vanilla, and walnuts, if desired. Don't worry that the mixture isn't really melding together. Set aside.

3. Put the evaporated milk and sugar in a large pot. Bring to a rolling boil and stir constantly for 10 minutes (a long-handled wooden spoon works best).

4. Turn off the heat. Add the chocolate-marshmallow mixture to the pot, stirring constantly until smooth and melted.

5. Pour the fudge mixture into the buttered baking pan and chill until firm, about an hour.

6. Remove the fudge from the fridge and let it stand until it reaches room temperature, then cut into 1-inch squares.

Marshmallow Nut Fudge

MAKES 100-PLUS SQUARES

INGREDIENTS

1 cup (2 sticks) unsalted butter, softened
16 ounces marshmallow creme
2 teaspoons vanilla extract
18 ounces (1 1/2 packages) semisweet chocolate chips
2 cups chopped walnuts
4 cups sugar
12 ounces evaporated milk

1. In a large bowl, mix the butter, marshmallow creme, and vanilla. Fold in the chocolate chips and walnuts.

2. In a large (6- to 8-quart) saucepan, combine the sugar and milk. Bring to a boil and cook for exactly 9 minutes, stirring constantly. Remove from the heat. (Caution: Do not leave unattended. If the mixture begins to boil over, turn down the heat.)

3. Add the hot milk and sugar to the butter mixture and stir until well blended.

4. Pour into a greased 13- by 9- by 2-inch baking pan and refrigerate for at least 3 hours. (The fudge can also be cooled in the freezer.) Cut into 1-inch squares, wrapping each in waxed paper, foil, or plastic wrap. This fudge can be stored at room temperature for a week. For longer storage, freeze.

Chocolate Turtles

MAKES APPROXIMATELY 5 DOZEN TURTLES

INGREDIENTS

2 cups chocolate chips,
milk or dark, divided
10 tablespoons (1 1/4 sticks)
unsalted butter, softened
to room temperature,
divided
14 ounces caramel candies
2 tablespoons milk
1 cup whole pecan halves

1. Line a 7- by 11-inch baking pan with foil and set aside. In a small microwavable bowl, place 1 cup of the chocolate chips and 1 tablespoon of the butter. Microwave repeatedly on medium high for 1-minute intervals until melted, stirring between timings.

2. Pour the mixture into the foil-lined pan and refrigerate for 15 to 20 minutes.

3. In a medium-size microwavable bowl, place the caramels, 1/2 cup of the butter, and the milk. Microwave repeatedly on medium high for 1-minute intervals, stirring between timings.

4. Stir in the pecans. Pour the mixture over the chilled chocolate.

5. Melt the remaining 1 cup chocolate chips and 1 tablespoon butter on medium-high heat as in step 1.

6. Spread this chocolate over the caramel layer and refrigerate for 1 to 2 hours. Turn the pan upside down onto a cutting board and remove the foil. Cut into 1-inch squares. Store in the refrigerator.

Homemade Jams

So easy to make, and the flavor of homemade jam is fantastic. Try it, and you may never go back to store-bought.

Rasberry Jam

MAKES 3 CUPS

INGREDIENTS
2 pounds fresh raspberries
(not too ripe)
4 cups (2 pounds) sugar

1. Place the raspberries in a saucepan and crush them slightly with a wooden spoon.

2. Cook over low heat until the fruit bubbles, stirring to keep it from sticking.

3. Add the sugar slowly; keep stirring until it dissolves.

4. Increase the heat, bringing the jam to a slow boil. Cook without stirring for 10 minutes, until the jam sets.

5. Ladle into warmed, sterilized jars and seal while the jam is hot, according to your canning jar manufacturer's directions.

Food is our common ground,
a universal experience.

Sheilah Graham

Homemade Jams

Strawberry Jam
MAKES 3 CUPS

INGREDIENTS
*2 pounds fresh
strawberries (not too
ripe)
Juice from 1 orange
4 cups (2 pounds) sugar
1 teaspoon butter*

1. Combine the strawberries and orange juice in a saucepan over low heat. Bring to a boil and cover; simmer for 15 minutes.

2. Mash gently with a potato masher or a whisk.

3. Add the sugar slowly; keep stirring until it dissolves.

4. Increase the heat, bringing the jam to a slow boil. Cook without stirring for 10 minutes, until the jam sets. Remove from the heat and stir in the butter.

5. Remove any scum. Ladle into warmed, sterilized jars and seal while the jam is hot, according to your canning jar manufacturer's directions.

Applesauce

MAKES 6 CUPS

INGREDIENTS
*8 medium-sized
    Macintosh apples*
*3/4 cup brown
    or white sugar*
*1 teaspoon
    ground cinnamon*
*1/4 cup water, apple juice,
    or lemonade*

1. Core and slice apples and place in large nonstick pot with remaining ingredients.

2. Cover and cook on low heat for 30-45 minutes, stirring every 5 minutes until sauce reaches desired consistency. Cook longer for a smoother sauce.

3. Remove skins with a fork.

4. Serve cool or warm, any time of day, with toast or pancakes, chicken or turkey, or vanilla ice cream.

DINNER

BAKED HAM

SERVES 15 TO 30

This is classic and has many benefits. It can feed a crowd, it requires virtually no preparation, and any leftovers will keep for a week—and you can use it for everything from sandwiches to omelets. When you get down to the bone, use it to flavor a big pot of pea soup (see page 72).

If you have a Polish or German meat market in your area, buy your ham there. Our favorite store for smoked hams in New York is Kurowycky in the East Village. Its hams are incomparable. Unfortunately, it doesn't sell via mail order. There are plenty of reputable hams available online, however. Nodine's (www.nodinesmokehouse.com) and Niman Ranch (www.nimanranch.com) are two excellent sources. (Do not, under any circumstances, use a canned ham for this recipe!)

This recipe is adapted from a collection by the editors of *Saveur* magazine, *Saveur Cooks Authentic American*. Scalloped potatoes (see page 248) are a traditional accompaniment. The rich, mild potatoes are a delicious counterpoint to the saltiness of the ham.

BAKED HAM

INGREDIENTS
*1 smoked ham (10 to 15
  pounds), on the bone
1 1/2 cups orange
  marmalade
1 cup Dijon mustard
1 1/2 cups packed
  brown sugar
2 tablespoons whole cloves*

1. Preheat the oven to 275 degrees.

2. Using a very sharp knife, score the skin of the ham into a crosshatch pattern. Place it in a roasting pan and cover lightly with foil. Roast for 2 hours. Remove from the oven and increase the heat to 350.

3. While the ham is roasting, combine the marmalade, mustard, and brown sugar in a medium bowl to use as a glaze.

4. Stud the ham with the cloves, placing one at the intersection of each crosshatch. Brush the surface of the ham with the glaze and return it to the oven. Bake for another hour, basting three or four times with the glaze. Allow the ham to rest for 20 minutes before carving. Serve warm or at room temperature.

PORK CHOPS WITH APPLES

SERVES 4

Most pork chops available in supermarkets these days are so lean, they lack the succulence we associate with pork. Ask your butcher to find meat that has been "sustainably raised" on a small-scale farm, and you'll get better results for your efforts in the kitchen.

INGREDIENTS

2 tablespoons vegetable oil
1 medium onion,
*   peeled and sliced*
4 pork chops, each 3/4-inch
*   to 1-inch thick*
Salt and pepper to taste
4 apples, peeled, cored,
*   and sliced*
2 tablespoons packed
*   brown sugar*
1/2 teaspoon dry mustard
1/8 teaspoon ground cloves
1 cup chicken broth
*   or water*

1. Preheat the oven to 350 degrees.

2. Heat the oil in a large skillet. Sauté the onion until soft and translucent, about 2 minutes. Remove the onion from the pan and set aside.

3. Add the pork chops to the pan and sauté briefly on each side to brown.

4. Put the chops into a 2-quart casserole dish, with a cover. Sprinkle the chops with salt and pepper, and add the apples and onion. In a small bowl, combine the brown sugar, mustard, cloves, and chicken broth or water. Pour this mixture over the chops. Cover and bake for 45 minutes. Alternatively, this can be done on top of the stove; be careful to monitor the heat.

BARBECUED RIBS

SERVES 4

Our friend Marty is a brilliant griller, and ribs are his specialty. I have known him to throw beer into this sauce, too! Half the fun is standing out back and talking politics while they cook. LT

INGREDIENTS
For the ribs:
2 tablespoons chili powder
Salt and pepper
2 (3-pound) racks
   of pork spare ribs

For the barbecue sauce:
3 cups ketchup
1 cup Heinz bottled
   chili sauce
Grated zest of 1 lemon
Juice of 2 large lemons
1/4 cup French's mustard
1 1/2 tablespoons
   Tabasco sauce
1/4 cup Worcestershire sauce
2 tablespoons molasses
2 tablespoons brown sugar
2 cloves garlic, chopped
1/4 cup chopped parsley
2 tablespoons
   apple cider vinegar
Salt and pepper to taste

1. Sprinkle the chili powder, salt, and pepper over the ribs and set aside.

2. In a saucepan, combine all of the barbecue sauce ingredients and warm through over low heat to blend the flavors. Set aside.

3. Prepare the grill: Ignite the charcoal and bank it on one side of the grill.

4. Place the ribs on the side of the grill without the coals, cover the grill (with the vents open, to keep the coals alive), and cook for an hour.

5. Baste the ribs with the barbecue sauce and continue cooking for 20 to 25 minutes, until done.

! Variation: You can also prepare these ribs in the oven. Preheat the oven to 325 degrees and place the ribs in a shallow baking pan. Bake in the center of the oven for 1 hour, depending on the ribs' size. Baste with sauce and cook for another half hour, until tender.

BEEF STEW

SERVES 4

This is a simple recipe that requires very little in order to produce superior results—but the little things are crucial. The quality of the meat itself is of the utmost importance. The cut should be chuck, rump, or round, preferably from grass-fed beef. The pieces of meat should be cut into 1 1/2- to 2-inch cubes—any smaller and you run the risk of overcooking the meat and drying it out. Last, the temperature must be kept very low. We prefer to cook stews in the oven in a covered casserole dish or enameled Dutch oven, because the heat is more easily controlled. A temperature of 250 to 300 degrees is perfect for a long, slow braise. This stew reheats well. It will keep refrigerated for three to four days.

INGREDIENTS

A few tablespoons of flour
3 pounds beef for stew (preferably chuck, rump, or the round), cut into 2-inch cubes
3 tablespoons olive oil or other vegetable oil, divided
1 large Spanish onion or 3 medium yellow onions, peeled and coarsely chopped
1 stalk celery, diced
1 clove garlic, peeled and flattened
1 bay leaf
1 sprig thyme or 1/2 teaspoon fresh thyme leaves

1. Preheat the oven to 300 degrees.

2. Put some flour on a plate. Dry the pieces of beef with a paper towel, then roll them in the flour to lightly coat. (Wondra flour happens to be very good for this, as well as for thickening sauces.)

3. Heat 2 tablespoons of the oil in a large, heavy frying pan. Sauté the meat, in batches, until it's browned on all sides. Do not crowd the pan; if you do, the meat will steam instead of brown. When the meat is finished cooking, put it into a heavy Dutch oven or casserole dish that has a cover.

4. Wipe the pan clean with a paper towel, then return it to the heat. Add the remaining tablespoon of oil and sauté the onion and celery until soft, about 7 minutes.

BEEF STEW

3 cups beef stock, beer, red
   or white wine, or water
   (or a combination)
6 carrots, peeled and
   cut into 2-inch lengths
3 medium potatoes, peeled
   and cut into large cubes

5. Add the onion, celery, garlic, herbs, and liquid to the Dutch oven, and place it in the oven. Check after 30 minutes. The liquid should be simmering gently. If it isn't, turn down the heat. After another hour, add the carrots and potatoes. Cook until the meat is fork-tender, about another hour.

6. Serve warm.

! Variations:
- Add a few tablespoons of chopped fresh or canned tomato, or a tablespoon of tomato paste.
- Add green beans, sautéed mushrooms, or peas for the last 30 minutes of cooking.
- Add a teaspoon of chopped fresh rosemary, a strip of orange rind, and some black olives for a Mediterranean flavor.

ROAST BEEF

SERVES 6 TO 8

Even if there are only two of you, buy the full amount of meat called for in this recipe. A larger roast is easier to cook to medium rare, and the leftovers make fabulous sandwiches with a dollop of horseradish and mayonnaise on a crusty roll. If you've never made Yorkshire pudding, you'll be amazed at how easy it is and wonder why you haven't done it before.

INGREDIENTS

For the Yorkshire pudding:
1 cup all-purpose flour
1 teaspoon salt
2 large eggs
1 cup whole milk
4 tablespoons vegetable oil or reserved beef fat from the roast

For the roast:
2 1/2 pounds russet potatoes, peeled and cut into 1-inch chunks
8 medium carrots, peeled and cut diagonally into 2-inch lengths
4 tablespoons extra-virgin olive oil, divided
1 3- to 3 1/4-pound beef eye of round roast
1 clove garlic, thinly sliced
Salt and pepper to taste

1. Make the batter for the Yorkshire pudding: In a blender, blend the flour, salt, eggs, and milk until just smooth. Chill the batter, covered, for at least 30 minutes.

2. Prepare the roast: Preheat the oven to 350 degrees. Toss the potatoes, carrots, and 3 tablespoons of the oil in a large bowl. Sprinkle with salt and pepper. Spread the vegetables in large roasting pan. Roast for 30 minutes.

3. With the point of a small knife, make small incisions in the meat. Insert garlic slices into the incisions. Sprinkle the roast with salt and pepper.

4. Push the vegetables to the sides of the pan, leaving space in the center. Place the roast in the center of the pan. Roast until a meat thermometer inserted into the center of the meat registers 125 degrees for medium rare—about 1 hour. Remove the roast from the oven and transfer it to a platter. Reserve 4 tablespoons of fat from the roast for the pudding, if desired. Tent the roast with foil and let it rest.

ROAST BEEF

5. Increase the oven temperature to 450 degrees. Spread out the vegetables again in the pan; continue roasting until they're tender and brown, about 10 minutes.

6. To bake the Yorkshire pudding, reduce the oven temperature to 425 degrees. Place a 9- by 13-inch baking dish in the oven and heat for 10 minutes. Add the oil or reserved beef drippings. Pour the prepared batter into the dish and bake for 20 to 25 minutes, or until golden brown. Serve immediately.

POT ROAST

SERVES 4 TO 6

INGREDIENTS

2 to 3 tablespoons
vegetable oil
2 large yellow onions,
chopped
2 to 3 cloves garlic, crushed
3 pounds lean beef brisket
Salt and pepper to taste
1 (28–ounce) can
plum tomatoes, crushed
6 medium-sized potatoes,
cut into quarters
4 to 6 large carrots,
peeled and quartered
Several handfuls fresh
green peas, or 1 package
frozen peas (optional)

1. Heat the oil in a Dutch oven or large stockpot.

2. Add the chopped onion and brown lightly. Add the garlic and sauté for 1 to 2 minutes.

3. Add the meat and brown on all sides over high heat, around 6 to 7 minutes. Add salt and pepper. Reduce the heat and add 1 ½ cups of water. Cover the pot tightly.

4. Simmer on low heat for 45 minutes.

5. Add the crushed tomatoes, cover again, and simmer while preparing the vegetables.

6. Stir the potatoes and carrots into the pot.

7. After meat has cooked a total of 2 hours, remove it carefully and lay it on a board. Slice thinly.

8. Return the meat to the pot and simmer for 1 hour, until everything is soft and tender.

9. During the last half hour, you can add fresh or defrosted peas, if you like.

10. Serve warm.

BRISKET

SERVES 12

A whole brisket will serve 12 people, with some left over for sandwiches the next day. Brisket is sold as an entire cut, but smaller pieces can be purchased; ask your butcher. No matter how large the cut of meat, make the same amount of marinade. The addition of gingersnaps may seem odd to some, but it's a traditional ingredient in sauerbraten. The spices in the cookies add some interesting flavors, and the flour helps to thicken the sauce.

INGREDIENTS

For the marinade:
1 (12-ounce) bottle of beer, any type
1 (18-ounce) bottle of barbecue sauce (we prefer mesquite-flavored)
1 envelope dried onion soup
6 gingersnap cookies, broken into pieces
2 tablespoons maple syrup

For the beef:
1 whole beef brisket (about 6 pounds)
1 medium onion, sliced

1. Combine all the marinade ingredients in a bowl and mix well.

2. Put the meat into a large roasting pan and add the sliced onion. Cover with marinade and pierce the meat with a fork. Cover the pan tightly with its lid (you can also use aluminum foil) and place it in the refrigerator overnight.

3. Remove from the fridge and let it come to room temperature (at least an hour).

4. Bake in a 325-degree oven for 4 hours.

5. Cool and slice the meat against the grain. Use the marinade for gravy.

NEW YORK STRIP STEAK

SERVES 2

New York Strip Steak is so-called because it used to be that the best cuts of beef were sent to New York. It came to mean steak that was well-marbled and top-grade, and cut from behind the short rib, where there is little muscle and high fat content. These days, it may also be called Kansas City strip, shell steak, sirloin club steak, or just plain old strip steak. Whatever you call it, it's delicious.

INGREDIENTS

Approximately 1 to 1 ½ pounds New York strip steak
1 garlic clove, cut in half
Coarse sea salt or kosher salt
1 teaspoon coarsely ground black pepper
2 tablespoons Worcestershire sauce
1 teaspoon Colman's dry mustard
1 teaspoon chili oil (less if desired)

1. Preheat the oven to broil.

2. Using either a fork or a small knife, stab the steak numerous times to create tiny perforations.

3. Rub both sides of the steak with the cut side of the garlic.

3. Coat both sides of the steak with coarse sea salt. Let it sit for 5 minutes.

4. Combine all the remaining ingredients and rub generously over the steak.

5. Broil for 3 to 5 minutes per side (for medium rare).

6. Let the steak rest for a few minutes, then slice thin against the grain and serve.

SHORT RIBS

SERVES 4

This dish is best if made the day before you plan to serve it.

INGREDIENTS
For the ribs:
4 pounds beef short ribs,
 on the bone
1 1/2 teaspoons salt
1 tablespoon freshly
 cracked black pepper
2 to 3 tablespoons olive oil
1 cup chopped onion
1/2 cup chopped and
 peeled carrots
1/2 cup chopped celery
1 teaspoon dried
 crushed thyme
2 bay leaves
2 tablespoons
 balsamic vinegar
1 1/2 cups port
2 1/2 cups red wine
4 cups beef stock
Several sprigs of parsley

1. Prepare the ribs: Preheat the oven to 325 degrees.

2. Rub the short ribs with salt and pepper.

3. Heat the oil in a large frying pan over a high flame. Add the ribs and brown on all sides, about 10 minutes total. Transfer the ribs to an oven-proof pan, bone-side up, in one layer, and set aside. Return the frying pan to the stove, reducing the heat to medium. Cook the onion, carrots, and celery until they all begin to caramelize. Add the thyme, bay leaves, vinegar, port, and red wine, and boil until reduced by half. Add the stock and parsley and bring just to a boil. Pour this mixture over the ribs.

4. Cover the pan very tightly (use foil if the pan doesn't have a cover, or use foil plus the cover if the cover doesn't fit tightly) and braise in the oven for 2 1/2 to 3 hours, or until the meat is quite tender, falling off the bone.

5. Remove the meat from the bone and place it in an oven-to-table casserole dish. Try to keep each rib in one piece.

SHORT RIBS

For the horseradish cream:
1/2 cup crème fraîche
2 tablespoons prepared (bottled) white horseradish
Salt and pepper

6. Using a sieve, strain the sauce over the meat in the casserole dish. (Discard the solids.) Cover and refrigerate the short ribs overnight. (This will allow the flavors to deepen, and you will be able to remove the grease that will rise to the surface and congeal.)

7. Remove the casserole from the refrigerator 1 1/2 hours before you plan to serve. Remove the fat from the surface of the casserole and discard.

8. Put the ribs into a preheated 300-degree oven to reheat. Taste for seasoning before serving.

9. Prepare the horseradish cream: Mix the horseradish with the crème fraîche, adding salt and pepper to taste. Warm in a saucepan on low to medium heat until just hot.

10. Serve the beef topped with sauce, with horseradish cream on the side.

CHILI AND CORNBREAD

SERVES 6

Legendary bad boy Billy the Kid once said, "Anybody who eats chili can't be that bad." Popularized on Texas cattle drives, chili's accompaniment, corn bread, was invented when early settlers learned how to use Indian cornmeal instead of wheat flour (which was hard to come by) in their breads, usually made in a Dutch oven. Baking it on top of the chili turns this into a true casserole, but you can make them separately as well. Or just make the chili and serve over rice.

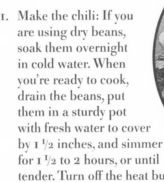

INGREDIENTS

For the chili:
1 cup dried red kidney beans or 3 cups canned cooked beans
1 teaspoon vegetable oil
1 pound ground beef, preferably ground round
2 yellow onions, diced
1 (14-ounce) bottle ketchup
2 (14.5-ounce) cans tomatoes
1/8 teaspoon cayenne pepper, or to taste
1/4 teaspoon chili powder, or to taste
Salt and pepper to taste

1. Make the chili: If you are using dry beans, soak them overnight in cold water. When you're ready to cook, drain the beans, put them in a sturdy pot with fresh water to cover by 1 1/2 inches, and simmer for 1 1/2 to 2 hours, or until tender. Turn off the heat but leave the beans in the water and add salt to taste. Set aside.

2. Add the vegetable oil to a large skillet set over medium heat. Add ground meat and onions, and cook until the meat has browned.

3. Add the ketchup, tomatoes, cayenne, chili powder, and salt and pepper to the skillet, and combine with the meat. Drain the beans.

CHILI AND CORNBREAD

For the corn bread topping:
1 ½ cups yellow cornmeal
½ cup all-purpose flour
2 teaspoons baking powder
1 teaspoon sugar
1 teaspoon salt
½ teaspoon baking soda
½ teaspoon chili powder
1 cup buttermilk
2 large eggs, beaten
1 (8-ounce) can
    creamed corn
½ cup shredded
    cheddar cheese
2 tablespoons vegetable oil

4. Transfer the meat mixture to a large casserole dish. Add the cooked beans and stir until well combined. (If you are using canned beans, drain them and rinse well under running water before adding them to the casserole.)

5. Heat the oven to 450 degrees.

6. Make the corn bread: In a large bowl, sift together the cornmeal, flour, baking powder, sugar, salt, baking soda, and chili powder.

7. In another bowl, combine the buttermilk, eggs, creamed corn, cheddar cheese, and vegetable oil. Add this mixture to the dry ingredients, mix until well combined. Then pour the corn-bread mixture over the chili in the casserole dish and spread it evenly over the top.

8. Bake for 20 minutes, until golden brown. Serve immediately.

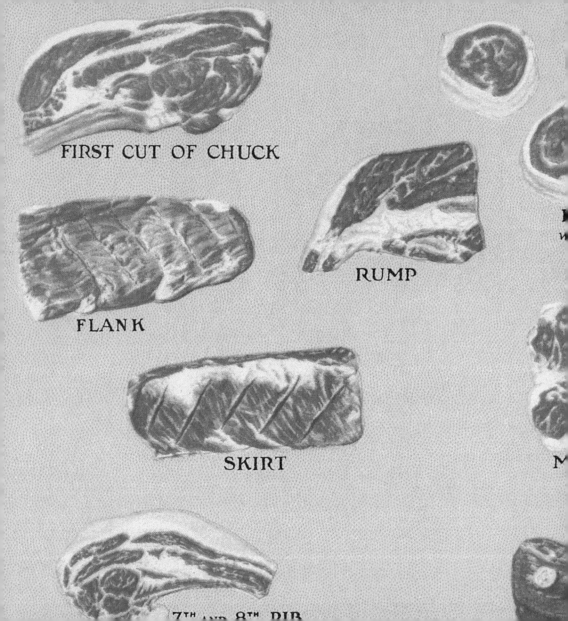

FIRST CUT OF CHUCK

FLANK

RUMP

SKIRT

7TH AND 8TH RIB

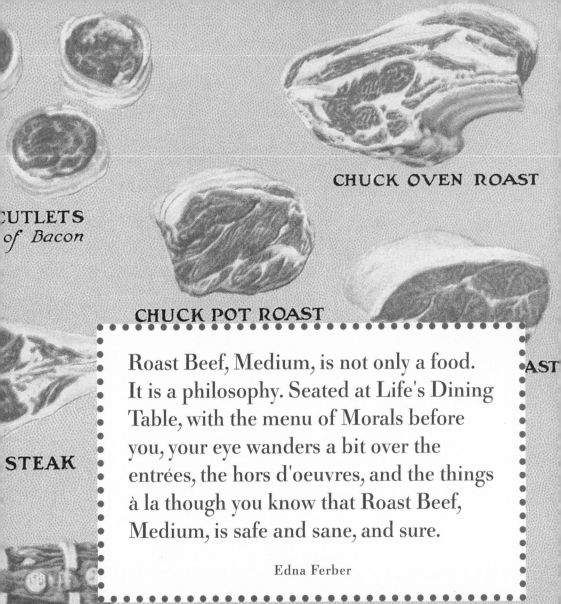

CHUCK OVEN ROAST

CUTLETS
of Bacon

CHUCK POT ROAST

AST

STEAK

Roast Beef, Medium, is not only a food. It is a philosophy. Seated at Life's Dining Table, with the menu of Morals before you, your eye wanders a bit over the entrées, the hors d'oeuvres, and the things à la though you know that Roast Beef, Medium, is safe and sane, and sure.

Edna Ferber

RICE AND BEANS

SERVES 4

The nutritional benefits of beans are undisputed, but that is secondary to how delicious and, indeed, comforting they can be. Serve with freshly steamed corn tortillas, some grated cheese, tomato salsa and a bowl of steaming rice, and you have the makings of a very satisfying vegetarian meal.

BEANS

INGREDIENTS
1 (16-ounce) bag dried black, red kidney, or pinto beans
1 bay leaf
Salt, to taste
¼ cup olive oil
1 large Spanish onion, chopped
4 cloves garlic, minced
1 large red or green bell pepper, seeded and diced
1 or 2 chipotle peppers, dried or "en adobo"
A few cups of chicken, beef, or vegetable broth (optional)
Red wine vinegar
Sugar

1. Rinse the beans and put them into a large pot. Add water to cover by 1 inch. Bring to a boil, turn off the heat, then let the beans sit for an hour. (Alternatively, you may wish to soak the beans overnight.)

2. Drain the beans and cover again with water. Add the bay leaf. Simmer over low heat until tender. This may take anywhere from 1 ½ to 3 hours, depending on the age of the beans. When the beans have softened but are not completely cooked, add salt to taste. (The beans will become as salty as the water they are cooked in. Do not add salt at the beginning of the cooking process—it will prevent the beans from cooking through.)

3. Put the olive oil into a medium-size frying pan over medium heat. Sauté the onion, garlic, and bell pepper until they're soft and the onion is translucent.

RICE AND BEANS

4. Drain the beans of most of their liquid, but leave enough so that you can continue to simmer them with their seasonings. Add the sautéed onion, garlic, and pepper; the chipotle pepper; and the optional broth, if you like. Simmer to blend the flavors. Add vinegar and sugar to taste before serving with boiled white rice.

RICE

INGREDIENTS
1 1/2 cups long grain white rice
1 teaspoon salt
1 tablespoon butter

1. Bring rice to a boil in the three cups of water, salt, and butter. Cover, turn heat down and simmer for 15 minutes.

2. Turn heat off and let rice stand for ten minutes.

! Variations:
- Add additional seasonings such as cumin and oregano for Mexican-style beans.
- Add a smoked ham hock to the beans while cooking, then shred the meat and add it to the beans when they're done.
- Add fresh, sautéed, or canned poblano chilies in place of the bell pepper.
- Add saffron to the rice while it's cooking and a splash of sherry to the beans for a Spanish accent.

CHICKEN FRIED STEAK

SERVES 4

This Southen favorite is devilishly good. Serve with mashed potatoes (see page 241) and collard greens (page 234), smothered in gravy, for the perfect down-home dinner.

INGREDIENTS
4 round steaks,
*   each ¹/₂ inch thick*
Salt and pepper
1 egg
¹/₄ cup milk
1 ¹/₂ cups all-purpose flour
Vegetable oil, for frying
1 cup heavy cream

1. Pound each steak with a mallet until it is ¹/₄ inch thick. Season with salt and pepper on each side.

2. Whisk together the egg and milk in a shallow bowl. Put the flour into another shallow bowl, and put a piece of waxed paper on the counter beside it.

3. Dip a steak into the flour, then into the egg mixture, then into the flour again; place the steak on the waxed paper. Repeat until all the steaks are coated. (Reserve 2 teaspoons of the flour to make the gravy later.)

4. Heat the cooking oil in a large, high-sided, heavy skillet over medium heat; it should be ¹/₂ inch deep. Flick a little flour into the pan—if it sizzles, the oil is ready.

CHICKEN FRIED STEAK

5. Fry the steaks on both sides until golden brown. Remove from the pan and place on paper towels to drain while you prepare the gravy.

6. Return the pan to the heat and add 2 tablespoons of the leftover dredging flour. Brown it, stirring constantly, then slowly add the heavy cream. Keep stirring over a low flame until thick. Scrape up any browned bits that are stuck to the pan. Taste the cream gravy and add salt and pepper to taste. Serve with the steaks.

! **Variation:** You can use mlk instead of heavy cream, if you wish.

HUNGARIAN GOULASH

SERVES 6

Contrary to popular belief, true *gulyas* does not include sour cream or tomato. What it does require, however, is genuine paprika, imported from Hungary. You can find it at specialty food stores, as well as many supermarkets. Some recipes recommend the addition of sauerkraut, which you can add at the very end, if desired. Serve with egg noodles.

INGREDIENTS
2 tablespoons butter
2 large onions,
*   peeled and chopped*
2 pounds beef or pork
*   for stew, cut into 1 ½- to*
*   2-inch cubes*
¼ teaspoon caraway seeds
½ teaspoon fresh or dried
*   marjoram leaves*
2 cloves garlic, minced
5 tablespoons imported
*   Hungarian paprika*
1 (14.5-ounce) can beef
*   stock*
1 cup water
4 large potatoes, peeled
*   and cut into chunks*

1. Melt the butter in a large pot over medium heat. Cook the onions until they are soft and translucent. Add the beef and brown it on all sides.

2. Add the caraway seeds, marjoram, garlic, and paprika. Cook for a minute or two to soften the garlic and release the flavor of the paprika. Add the beef broth and water, and cover.

3. Simmer the beef over very low heat for 2 hours. (Alternatively, use an oven-proof casserole and cook the goulash in a 300-degree oven.)

4. Add the potatoes and cook until they are tender, about an hour. Season to taste and serve.

STUFFED CABBAGE

SERVES 6

While stuffed cabbage is typically considered to be classic Slavic peasant food, many cultures have their own versions of "stuffed leaves." Large leaves of Swiss chard can be used instead of cabbage. This recipe is adapted from the Time Life cookbook *Pork*, from the Good Cook series. It tastes even better if it's made the day before and reheated in the oven.

INGREDIENTS

1 large head white or savoy cabbage
2 medium onions, peeled and finely chopped
2 tablespoons vegetable oil
2 tablepoons raw long-grain rice
2 tablespoons mixed fresh parsley, dill, and thyme
Salt and pepper to taste
1 ½ pounds finely chopped or ground boneless pork, beef, lamb, or a mixture
1 large slice sourdough or other sturdy bread, soaked in water and squeezed dry
1 pound sauerkraut, drained, with juice reserved
A few tablespoons tomato puree or juice sour cream, for garnish

1. Put a large pot of salted water on the stove over high heat. Core the cabbage. When the water comes to a boil, plunge the cabbage into the water and turn off the heat. Let it sit for half an hour, until you can easily detach 24 large leaves. Cut the hard center rib out of each leaf and set the leaves aside while you prepare the filling.

2. In a heavy skillet, sauté the onions in the oil until they are soft. Add the rice and stir until the rice is coated with the oil and begins to turn opaque. Stir in the herbs and season with salt and pepper.

STUFFED CABBAGE

3. In a bowl, combine the onion mixture and the pork with the soaked bread. Work the mixture with your hands until it has a smooth consistency and is well combined.

4. Make the rolls: Spread each cabbage leaf out flat. Place a bit of stuffing in the center. Fold in the sides, and then roll up. A 2- to 3-inch roll isn't too small! You should be able to make 18 to 24 rolls.

5. Line the bottom of a large casserole with a layer of sauerkraut. Put in a layer of cabbage rolls, then a layer of sauerkraut, and continue, ending with a layer of sauerkraut.

6. Mix the sauerkraut juice with the tomato, pour over the rolls, cover and bake in a 300-degree oven for 1 1/2 to 2 hours, until the pork has cooked through. The leaves may be refrigerated and reheated the next day.

7. Serve with some sour cream on the side.

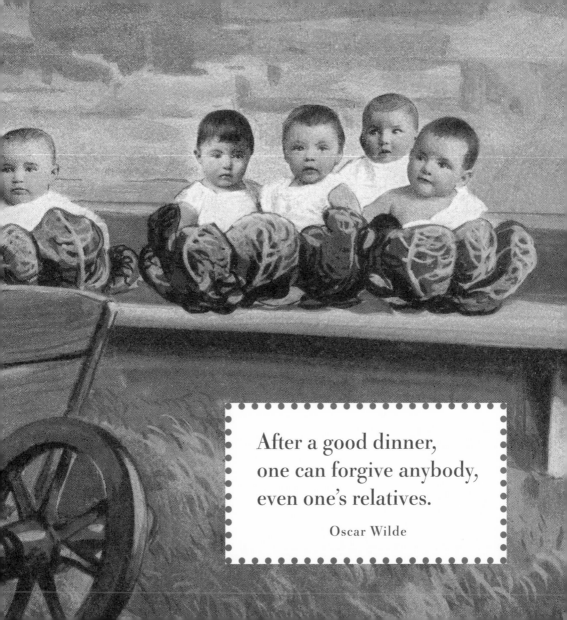

After a good dinner,
one can forgive anybody,
even one's relatives.

Oscar Wilde

SHEPHERD'S PIE

SERVES 6

This takes some prep time but then goes in the oven for 40 minutes, which gives you plenty of time with family or friends before sitting down to dinner.

INGREDIENTS

For the lamb-and-vegetable filling:

1 pint (2 cups) pearl onions (about 10 ounces)
2 pounds boneless lamb, cut into 1-inch cubes
Salt and pepper
5 tablespoons all-purpose flour, divided
3 ½ tablespoons butter, divided
½ cup white wine
2 tablespoons tomato paste
1 cup beef stock
1 cup water
2 teaspoons chopped fresh thyme
5 carrots, peeled and cut into 1-inch pieces
1 cup fresh or frozen peas

1. Prepare the filling: Preheat the oven to 350 degrees.

2. Blanch the onions in boiling water for 2 to 3 minutes, then transfer them to a bowl of ice water. Drain the onions. To peel, trim off the root end and squeeze each onion out of its skin. Reserve.

3. Pat the lamb dry using paper towels, and season with salt and pepper. Place 3 tablespoons of the flour into a paper or plastic bag, add the lamb, and shake to coat all sides of the lamb cubes.

4. In an oven-proof casserole or pot, melt 2 tablespoons of the butter and brown the lamb in it. Remove the lamb and set aside.

5. Add the wine to deglaze the bottom of the pan, being careful to stir up the brown bits. Stir in the tomato paste and add the stock, water, thyme, carrots, reserved onions, and lamb. Bring to a simmer over high heat, then cover the pot with a lid or foil (or both) and transfer to the preheated oven. Cook for 1 ½ to 2 hours, stirring several times, until the lamb is tender. Add the peas and salt and pepper to taste.

SHEPHERD'S PIE

**For the mashed
potato topping:**
2 pounds russet potatoes
1/2 to 3/4 cup whole milk or
    half-and-half, warmed
3 tablespoons butter
Salt and pepper to taste

6. Meanwhile, make the topping: Peel and quarter the potatoes. Cook them in salted water until tender, about 20 to 25 minutes.

7. Drain the potatoes and put them through a ricer or mash by hand. Gradually stir in the warm milk, butter, salt, and pepper.

8. Assemble and bake the pie: If the sauce needs thickening, melt remaining 1 1/2 tablespoons of butter with the remaining 2 tablespoons of flour in small saucepan. Little by little, whisk in a cup of sauce from the lamb and bring to a simmer, continuing to whisk occasionally until the sauce has thickened. Return the thickened sauce to the lamb. Preheat the oven to 375 degrees. Adjust the rack to the middle of the oven.

9. Place the lamb mixture into a decorative oven-proof casserole dish and top with mashed potatoes. Decorate the top with the tines of a fork.

10. Bake until the meat and casserole are thoroughly heated through and the mashed potatoes have browned on top, about 40 minutes. If the potatoes don't brown sufficiently, place under the broiler for a few minutes.

CLASSIC MEATLOAF WITH GRAVY

SERVES 6

Meatloaf has been an American staple since the early 1900s. There are so many wonderful variations, but when it comes to the classic, we don't think you'll find a better recipe than this one.

INGREDIENTS

For the meatloaf:
2 pounds ground beef,
*   preferably ground round*
1/2 cup diced yellow onions
2 tablespoons finely
*   chopped parsley*
1 1/2 tablespoons
*   Worcestershire sauce*
1 egg
1/2 (10 3/4 ounce) can cream
*   of mushroom soup*
1 clove garlic, finely chopped
1 teaspoon salt-free
*   seasoning (such as Mrs.*
*   Dash Table Blend or*
*   Trader Joe's 21*
*   Seasoning Salute)*
1/4 cup ketchup
4 slices bacon
1/4 cup red wine

For the gravy:
*   1 to 2 tablespoons flour*
*   1/4 cup beef broth*
*   1/2 10 3/4 ounce can*
*   cream of mushroom*
*   soup*
*   Salt and pepper*

1. Make the meatloaf: Preheat the oven to 350 degrees.

2. In a large bowl, mix the meat, onions, parsley, Worcestershire sauce, egg, mushroom soup, garlic, and seasoning together with your hands.

3. Press the mixture into a loaf shape. Transfer into a medium-size casserole dish so that the meat loaf sits in the middle with room on the sides.

4. Cover the top of the meat with the ketchup, lay the bacon strips on top, and pour the wine into the bottom of the dish.

5. Bake uncovered for 1 hour. Drain the drippings into a saucepan, return the meat loaf to the oven, and broil for 5 minutes, until the bacon is sizzling.

6. Make the gravy: While the meat loaf broils, heat the drippings over a medium flame, whisking in as much flour as there are drippings. When the gravy bubbles, whisk in the broth and mushroom soup. Continue stirring until thick (approximately 5 minutes). Season to taste and serve.

SWEDISH MEATBALLS WITH GRAVY

MAKES 50 MEATBALLS; SERVES 4 (GENEROUSLY)

When my mother brought us from Sweden to Hollywood, I was three and my nanny came along. Nanny was a great baker, but her meatballs were divine. Small and served with lingonberry preserves (every supermarket offers these berries now—you can usually find them where the marmalades are), mashed potatoes, and often spinach, which, despite Popeye's popularity at the time, I did not like. These meatballs are easy but it does take some time to make enough of them! LT

MEATBALLS

INGREDIENTS
1 1/2 tablespoons olive oil
*1 small yellow onion,
   minced (around 3 tablespoons)*
*1 pound ground sirloin,
   very lean*
*1 1/2 tablespoons
   Worcestershire sauce*
1/2 cup half-and-half
2 tablespoons ketchup
1 large egg
1 teaspoon salt
1/4 teaspoon black pepper
1/2 cup bread crumbs
1 tablespoon butter
1/2 cup water

1. Heat the oil in a small skillet over medium heat. Add the onion and cook until just soft but not brown, about 5 minutes. Let cool.

2. In a large bowl, combine the beef, Worcestershire sauce, half-and-half, ketchup, cooked onion, egg, salt, and pepper. Mix with clean hands to blend.

3. Add the bread crumbs to the meat and mix well. With wet hands (to keep the meat from sticking), form the mixture into small balls about 1 1/4 inches in diameter. If the mixture is too soft, add more bread crumbs.

4. Place the meatballs on a plate brushed with cold water. Heat a large skillet over a medium-high flame, melt the butter, and add as many meatballs as there is room for them to roll around. Brown on all sides, about 5 minutes.

SWEDISH MEATBALLS WITH GRAVY

5. Add the water to the pan, turn down the heat, cover, and simmer for 5 minutes. Remove the meatballs to a plate.

6. Repeat steps 3 through 5 until all the meatballs are done.

GRAVY

INGREDIENTS
3 tablespoons butter
1 shallot, minced
1 tablespoon minced
  red pepper
2 cups chicken broth
½ cup heavy cream
¾ cup lingonberry
  preserves (optional;
  you can also serve
  on the side)

1. Return the meatball-browning skillet to the heat, adding the butter, shallot, and red pepper.

2. Sauté until softened and golden brown. Add the chicken broth and heavy cream.

3. Stir in the preserves and simmer just until hot. Return the meatballs to the pan to coat them with gravy. Serve.

SPAGHETTI AND MEATBALLS

SERVES 6

INGREDIENTS

For the spaghetti sauce:
3 tablespoons olive oil
1 medium onion, diced
1 stalk celery, diced
1 carrot, peeled and diced
4 cloves garlic, minced
1 (28-ounce) can crushed
   or diced tomatoes
1 (8-ounce) can
   tomato sauce
1/2 teaspoon fresh or a big
   pinch of dried oregano
1/4 teaspoon fresh or
   a pinch of dried thyme
Salt and pepper

1. Prepare the sauce: In a 2 1/2 - to 3-quart pot, heat the oil over medium-high heat. Add the onion, celery, and carrot, and cook until softened, about 5 minutes. Add the garlic and cook for about 1 minute. Stir in the tomatoes, tomato sauce, oregano, and thyme, and season with salt and pepper. Bring to a boil, lower the heat, and simmer, covered, for 25 minutes.

2. Prepare the meatballs: Put the bread into a small bowl, with milk to cover.

3. In a large bowl, mix the beef, egg, cheese, garlic, and parsley.

4. Squeeze the excess milk from the bread and mash with a fork.

5. Add the bread to the beef mixture and combine well with your hands.

6. Shape meatballs as round as you can, about the size of golf balls, and place them on a platter.

7. Heat the oil in a large heavy skillet until medium hot.

SPAGHETTI AND MEATBALLS

For the meatballs:
*1 ½ cups of cubed
   or shredded bread,
   preferably a few days old
Milk, enough to cover bread
1 pound ground beef
1 egg
⅓ cup grated
   Parmesan cheese
1 clove garlic, minced
A few teaspoons chopped
   fresh parsley leaves
¼ cup olive oil, for frying*

For the pasta:
1 pound spaghetti

8. Add the meatballs to the hot oil. Do not crowd the skillet; cook in batches if necessary.

9. Brown the meatballs well on all sides and remove to paper towels to drain as they are done. The meatballs should have a crisp brown crust.

10. Assemble the dish: Add the meatballs to the tomato sauce and simmer, uncovered, for up to 3 hours. Add a little water if the sauce becomes too thick.

11. Prepare the spaghetti according to package instructions and serve with the meatballs and sauce.

VEGETARIAN LASAGNA

SERVES 8 TO 10

This is a great dish to prepare ahead of time. Just put it into the oven an hour before dinner and then sit down to make the most of your time with your loved ones. Add a simple salad and some great bread, and your meal is complete.

INGREDIENTS
1 pound lasagna noodles
2 tablespoons olive oil
10 ounces ricotta cheese
 (part-skim or nonfat
 ricotta may be
 substituted)
1 cup pesto sauce
6 cups chopped
 raw spinach
4 to 5 cups tomato sauce,
 homemade or
 store-bought
1 cup tomato paste
3 cups shredded
 mozzarella cheese
 (part-skim or nonfat
 mozzarella may be
 substituted)

1. Preheat the oven to 350 degrees.

2. In a large stockpot, bring 6 to 8 cups water to a boil. Add the pasta and oil; let the noodles cook for approximately 8 minutes.

3. While the pasta cooks, mix the ricotta cheese, pesto sauce, and spinach in a large bowl. Set aside.

4. In a large saucepan, heat the tomato sauce and tomato paste, stirring until blended. Turn off the heat and set aside.

5. Drain the pasta and begin assembly: In a 13- by 9-inch baking dish, spread, in order, a thin layer of sauce, pasta, half of the ricotta mixture, sauce, pasta, sauce, 1 cup mozzarella, pasta, the remaining half of the ricotta mixture, sauce, pasta, sauce, 1 cup mozzarella, pasta, and sauce. Finally, top with remaining mozzarella.

6. Cover with aluminum foil and bake for approximately 45 minutes. Remove the foil and bake for another 10 minutes. Let the lasagna stand for at least 10 minutes before serving.

LASAGNA WITH MEAT SAUCE

SERVES 8 TO 10

When Natasha and I were kids, birthdays were synonymous with our Mom's homemade lasagna. I loved helping her "build" the lasagna, one meaty, cheesy layer at a time. And by the age of nine or ten, I could make this lasagna blindfolded. It's the perfect one-dish meal to serve a gaggle of pint-size picky eaters. But it also happens to be a timeless hit with grown-ups. I believe it's what they call a crowd pleaser. KF

INGREDIENTS
For the sauce:
Extra-virgin olive oil
1 pound lean ground beef
2 medium-size onions,
*   finely chopped*
1 cup sliced mushrooms
6 to 8 cloves garlic,
*   finely chopped*
6 medium tomatoes,
*   fresh or canned*
1 (28-ounce) can
*   crushed tomatoes*
1 (5.5-ounce) can
*   tomato paste*
2 teaspoons
*   balsamic vinegar*
2 tablespoons ketchup
1 teaspoon dried oregano

1. First, make the sauce: Heat 1 tablespoon of the olive oil over medium-high heat and sauté the ground beef until it's browned, about 3 minutes. Pour off the fat and set aside.

2. In a large non-aluminum pot over medium-high heat, sauté the onions in 2 tablespoons of olive oil until the onions soften, about 3 minutes. Add the mushrooms and garlic and sauté until the mushrooms are tender, about 2 more minutes. Add the rest of the sauce ingredients, including the reserved beef, and bring to a boil. Turn down the heat and simmer for an hour.

3. While the sauce is simmering, put a large pot of water on the stove to boil. (It should be large enough to accommodate the spinach.) Plunge the fresh spinach into the boiling water and cook for 3 to 4 minutes, or until all of the spinach is wilted. Drain in a colander. When it's cool enough to handle, squeeze as much liquid as possible out of the spinach, then chop. (If you're using frozen

LASAGNA WITH MEAT SAUCE

¼ cup finely chopped fresh
   basil (dried oregano is
   fine—it retains its
   punch—but dried basil
   does not)
Salt and pepper to taste

For the lasagna:
1 bag spinach, well washed,
   or 1 box frozen, chopped
   spinach, approximately
   6-8 ounces
1 pound ricotta cheese
Salt and pepper to taste
1 ½ pounds
   fresh mozzarella
1 (8-ounce) package
   no-boil lasagna noodles
¼ cup grated Parmesan
   cheese

spinach, follow the package directions, then drain and proceed as above.) In a small bowl, combine the spinach with the ricotta. Add salt and pepper to taste. Set aside. Thinly slice the mozzarella.

4. Oil a 13- by 9-inch baking dish. Spread a quarter of the sauce on the bottom of the dish, then place four or five of the dried sheets of pasta on top of the sauce. Spread a third of the ricotta-spinach mixture over the pasta. Continue to layer the other ingredients, using a third of the sliced mozzarella, then a quarter of the sauce. Top with one final layer of pasta, the rest of the sauce, and the mozzarella. Sprinkle with Parmesan. Cover loosely with aluminum foil.

5. Preheat the oven to 375 degrees and bake for an hour. Carefully uncover and let stand for 5 minutes before serving. The lasagna may be assembled a day ahead of time and refrigerated until you are ready to bake it.

FETTUCCINE ALFREDO

SERVES 4 TO 6

This is one of those wonderfully comforting pasta dishes that you can make in a flash after a busy day at work. Fresh fettuccine, especially homemade, brings this dish to another level. A side of steamed asparagus with a squeeze of lemon, and a loaf of Italian bread make this simple dinner simply elegant.

INGREDIENTS
1 tablespoon salt
1 cup heavy cream
5 tablespoons butter, divided
1 cup freshly grated
*   Parmesan cheese*
1/4 teaspoon salt
Dash of white pepper
*   (or black if you don't*
*   have white)*
Dash of nutmeg
2 tablespoons chopped
*   fresh parsley*
1 pound fettuccine,
*   dried or fresh*
Extra Parmesan and
*   parsley, for garnish*

1. Put a large pot of water onto the stove to boil. Add the salt.

2. In a large skillet over medium heat, simmer the cream with 3 tablespoons of the butter for about 5 minutes, until the cream is reduced and somewhat thickened. Turn off the heat.

3. Add the Parmesan, salt, pepper, nutmeg, and parsley to the cream, and stir.

4. When the water comes to a boil, add the fettuccine and cook according to package directions. The pasta should be firm in the middle ("al dente") and not mushy.

5. Return the pasta to the pot and toss with the remaining 2 tablespoons of butter; add the cream mixture and toss again. Divide among pasta bowls, sprinkle with additional Parmesan and parsley, and serve.

MACARONI AND CHEESE

SERVES 6 TO 8 AS A MAIN DISH, 12 TO 16 AS A SIDE

We know you are addicted to the stuff in the box, but try this and we promise, you'll never go back. We have made it for parties and never had any left. It takes a little bit of work to make the white sauce that serves as the base for this recipe, but it is well worth the effort. We once made this recipe with really expensive cheese that we hand-grated—which was a bit messy and time consuming. The next time, we used a bag of inexpensive pre-grated cheese, which took no time at all. Both versions tasted the same.

INGREDIENTS
For the sauce and pasta:
1 pound elbow macaroni
1 teaspoon olive oil
4 tablespoons butter
4 tablespoons
  all-purpose flour
3 cups whole milk
¾ cup heavy cream
1 pound shredded cheddar
  or Monterey Jack cheese
4 teaspoons Dijon mustard
1 ½ teaspoons salt
Ground pepper, to taste

For the topping:
3 cups packaged croutons,
  any flavor you like
2 tablespoons butter,
  melted
4 ounces shredded
  cheddar cheese

1. Preheat the oven to 400 degrees. Butter a large, shallow baking dish.

2. Cook the macaroni in a large pot of boiling salted water with the oil until it's tender but still a bit firm in the middle ("al dente"). Drain the pasta, reserving 1 cup of its cooking water.

3. While the pasta is cooking, melt the butter in a heavy pot over low heat.

4. Whisk in the flour and cook, continuing to whisk, for about 5 minutes. Whisk in a few tablespoons of the milk (to ensure that lumps don't form), then whisk in the rest of the milk in a slow, steady stream. Bring to a boil, whisking the whole time. When the sauce starts to boil, turn the heat to simmer and continue whisking for 2 more minutes.

MACARONI AND CHEESE

5. Stir in the cream, cheese, mustard, salt, and pepper. Remove from the heat and pour over the macaroni. Add the cup of reserved cooking water. Mix and transfer to the baking dish. (Note: The mixture will be runny. Not to worry!)

6. Make the topping: Crush the croutons while they're still in the bag and empty the crumbs into a bowl. Add the melted butter and the cheese, and mix.

7. Sprinkle the topping over the dish and bake for about 30 minutes, until bubbling and brown on top. Serve while hot.

BAKED ZITI

SERVES 4

When it comes to eating, I am a serious creature of habit. If I find something I really like, I stick. So it's not unusual for me to become addicted to a particular dish and eat it day after day until eventually I either bore of it or make a new delicious discovery. I offer this information as background to my love affair with Baked Ziti—one of the all-time great comfort foods of my youth. The romance began in my 9th year and ended in my 11th, when Ziti was finally usurped by the ubiquitous Chinese Sparerib. But for those two years, Baked Ziti and I spent no less than three evenings a week together. Ordered in by phone from the local pizzeria, where they knew me by name—okay, they knew me by *voice*—a huge steaming container of pasta accompanied by a fat piece of buttery garlic bread arrived at our door in twenty minutes. The penne was piled high in a cushion of ricotta cheese and hearty marinara sauce, and topped with gooey fresh mozzarella. It was messy, tummy warming, and irresistible. I weighed in at under 90 pounds in those days, but I will swear on the *Joy of Cooking*, I never left a bite or crumb uneaten. The following recipe is the closest I've ever come to replicating that cherished childhood favorite. KF

INGREDIENTS
1 pound ziti
1 recipe Basic Tomato
 Sauce (follows)
½ cup freshly grated
 Parmigiano-Regiano
 cheese
1 cup whole-milk ricotta
 cheese, with salt and
 pepper added to taste
1 (10-ounce) ball
 whole-milk mozzarella
 cheese, cut into small
 pieces
1 teaspoon butter

1. Follow the directions on the package for cooking the ziti, but err on the side of undercooking. The pasta must be quite firm to start, as it will cook further in the sauce.

2. In a large bowl, combine the pasta with three-quarters of the sauce. Stir in the Parmesan, the ricotta, and about half of the mozzarella.

3. Rub a baking dish with the butter. Put the pasta mixture in. Top with the remaining mozzarella and remaining sauce and bake in a 425-degree oven, uncovered, for about 25 minutes. If desired, place under the broiler to brown the top.

4. Remove from oven and serve immediately.

BASIC TOMATO SAUCE

MAKES ENOUGH SAUCE FOR I POUND OF PASTA, OR ABOUT TWO AND A HALF CUPS

We don't think we've ever made tomato sauce the same way twice, depending on available time and what's in the fridge. Sometimes we add chopped carrot or eliminate the garlic. You can add hot red chili flakes, chopped fresh or dried basil, thyme, parsley, oregano, or any combination. Of course, if it is summer and you have great fresh tomatoes on hand, use them.

INGREDIENTS
2 tablespoons olive oil
1 medium yellow onion,
    chopped very fine
1 stalk celery,
    chopped very fine
1 clove garlic, minced
½ bay leaf
1 teaspoon salt
pepper to taste
1 (28-ounce) can whole
    plum tomatoes in juice
    or 2 ¼ cups fresh
    tomatoes, peeled,
    quartered, and seeded

1. Sauté the onion and celery in the oil over medium heat until soft. Add the garlic and sauté for another few minutes until light golden. Add the salt, pepper, bay leaf, and the juice from the canned tomatoes. Simmer for a few minutes, squeeze the remaining tomatoes into pulp with your hands and add.

2. Bring the mixture to a boil, then reduce the heat and simmer over low heat, uncovered, stirring occasionally, for half an hour or longer, until the sauce reaches your desired thickness. The longer and slower it cooks, the better.

3. If you prefer a very smooth sauce, pass the sauce (removing the bay leaf first) through a food mill or blend it in batches in a blender. Taste again and adjust the seasoning.

PIZZA

YIELDS 1 PIZZA (SERVES 4 TO 6)

If you are a perfectionist, you will need a pizza stone for this recipe. They are readily available at specialty cookware shops. But we like the results you get with a cookie sheet as well.

INGREDIENTS

For the dough:
1 teaspoon active dry yeast
2/3 cup warm water
2 cups
all-purpose flour
1 teaspoon salt
2 tablespoons olive oil
Oil for bowl
Cornmeal for the
*   pizza stone*

For the toppings:
1 cup tomato sauce
1/2 pound mozzarella,
*   shredded*
1/2 cup grated
*   Romano cheese*
1 tablespoon dried basil
1 tablespoon dried oregano
1 teaspoon dried red
pepper flakes

1. Prepare the crust: Preheat the oven to 475 degrees.

2. Sprinkle the yeast over the warm water and let it stand for 1 minute. Stir until the yeast dissolves.

3. In a large bowl, combine the flour, salt, and olive oil. Stir in the water-yeast mixture until a soft dough forms. Knead for 5 minutes, adding more flour if the dough gets too sticky or wet.

4. Coat a bowl with additional olive oil and place the dough inside, covering with plastic wrap. Let this rise for 1 1/2 hours.

5. Flatten the dough on a floured work surface and roll it out to a 12-inch circle. If you get inspired, toss it in the air a few times, trying to catch the edges; this helps to stretch the dough and creates a nice elasticity. It's also easier than rolling.

6. Place the dough on a pizza stone or cookie sheet that has been dusted with cornmeal.

7. Assemble the pizza: Spread the sauce almost to the edge of the dough and cover it with the mozzarella, grated Romano cheese, basil, oregano, and red pepper flakes. Bake it on the bottom shelf of the oven for 12 to 15 minutes, or until it's crisp and the cheese is bubbly.

ROAST TURKEY WITH GIBLET GRAVY

SERVES 10 TO 12

Everybody has a trick for producing the perfect bird. Ours is simple: Baste every 15 to 20 minutes and roast at a relatively low heat. And, of course, it's important to start with a bird that hasn't been frozen. Buy fresh and buy organic if at all possible.

INGREDIENTS
1 turkey (approximately 14 pounds)
2 lemons with the skin sliced off
1 stick (8 tablespoons) butter
5 cups chicken stock
1 tablespoon all-purpose flour
1 teaspoon cornstarch

1. Preheat the oven to 450 degrees.

2. Remove the giblets from the turkey cavity and set aside. Rinse and dry the turkey, and rub it inside and out with the lemons.

3. Slice the stick of butter into thin pieces and place all over the outside of the turkey. Stuff the turkey with prepared, cooled dressing (see page 239). (Do not use warm stuffing, and do not stuff the turkey ahead of time. Doing either of these can promote the growth of dangerous bacteria.)

4. Put the turkey into a roasting pan and pour the chicken stock around it. Add the giblets to the pan. Put the bird into the oven and bake for 20 minutes.

ROAST TURKEY WITH GIBLET GRAVY

5. Turn the heat down to 375 degrees and baste every 15 minutes for just over 5 hours (20 minutes per pound). If it gets too brown, cover loosely with aluminum foil.

6. Remove the turkey from the oven and transfer to a carving board. Let it rest for 20 minutes.

7. Remove as much fat as possible from the pan. Pour ½ cup of the remaining pan juices into a saucepan. Whisk in the flour and cornstarch. When smooth, add the rest of the pan juices and heat over a medium flame, stirring until thickened. Taste for seasoning.

8. Remove the stuffing from the turkey and carve.

! **Variation:** You can add up to ½ cup of half and half, heavy cream, or milk at the end of step 7 to extend the gravy and make it a little richer.

TURKEY MEATLOAF

SERVES 6

We never had meatloaf growing up, but these days, turkey meatloaf is a staple for my husband and me. It's healthy, delicious, and above all, comforting, on a chilly winter night. I make one on Sunday and it lasts us all week. Serve it with Smashed Red Potatoes (see page 245) and a salad for a meal that's both healthy and hearty. NTF

INGREDIENTS

1 medium onion, minced
1 stalk celery, minced
1 carrot, minced
1 tablespoon olive oil
1 1/2 pounds ground turkey
1/2 cup dry bread crumbs
1 large egg
6 tablespoons ketchup,
  plus 1/3 cup for topping
2 cloves garlic, minced
2 tablespoons club soda
1/4 teaspoon salt
1/4 teaspoon pepper

1. Preheat the oven to 350 degrees.

2. Sauté the onion, celery, and carrot in the olive oil until the onion is translucent.

3. Combine the sautéed vegetables with the remaining ingredients in a large bowl. Mix well, then shape into a loaf and place on a foil-lined sheet pan, or press the mixture into a 9- by 5- by 3-inch loaf pan or a casserole dish. Spread 1/3 cup ketchup over the top.

4. Bake for 50 minutes, until thoroughly cooked.

CHICKEN STEW

SERVES 10 TO 12

This is an easy dinner for a crowd. Serve with Garlic Bread (see page 222).

INGREDIENTS

3 ½ pounds boneless,
skinless chicken breasts,
cut into 1-inch cubes
Salt and pepper
⅓ cup all-purpose flour
9 tablespoons olive oil,
divided
2 cups dry white wine
2 yellow onions,
peeled and chopped
2 cups chicken broth
1 (28.5-ounce) can Italian
plum tomatoes, seeded
and chopped
1 (1-pound) package
baby carrots
3 to 4 sprigs each of
rosemary and thyme
and 6 stems parsley,
tied together
1 (8-ounce) package
mushrooms
1 (10-ounce) bag frozen
peas

1. Season the chicken with salt and pepper and then toss with the flour.

2. Heat 3 tablespoons of the oil in a large skillet over medium-high heat and brown a third of the chicken. Repeat until all of the chicken has been cooked. Remove to a bowl or platter. Add the white wine to the skillet to deglaze the pan. Scrape up the browned bits from the bottom of the pan and simmer to reduce the wine by half.

3. In a 3-quart saucepan, sauté the onions until translucent. Add the reduced wine, broth, tomatoes, carrots, and herbs. Cover and simmer over low heat for 30 minutes.

4. Add the chicken, mushrooms, and peas, and simmer for another 10 minutes. Discard the herbs and serve!

ULTIMATE ROAST CHICKEN

SERVES 4

When I was first married, my husband taught me this recipe. It came from his first wife's mother. I make it often; the only change I've made in the last 30 years is to buy organic chickens. I also learned how to make gravy, which I could never master before. I always serve this dish with Swedish lingonberries (but cranberries are great, too), sometimes stuffing it with doctored-up Pepperidge Farm Herb Seasoned Stuffing (see page 239). Or I serve it with jasmine rice and a green salad with dried cranberries, walnuts, and sliced pears. LT

INGREDIENTS

1 whole roasting chicken (4 to 5 pounds), preferably organic
1 large lemon (slice off all the skin and cut in half)
Stuffing (optional—follow directions on package to prepare)
10 tablespoons butter, divided
1 cup white wine
1 heaping tablespoon all-purpose flour

1. Preheat the oven to 425 degrees.

2. Remove the liver and giblets from the cavity of the chicken. Put them in a small saucepan, cover with cold water, and simmer for an hour.

3. Squeeze the lemon juice all over the chicken, including the inside. (If you aren't stuffing the chicken, leave the lemon halves themselves inside the cavity.)

4. If you are stuffing the bird, do it now.

5. Cut 8 tablespoons (1 stick) of the butter into thin slices. Put these slices all over the outside of the bird—like little solar panels.

6. Put the chicken into the oven. After 15 minutes, turn the temperature down to 350 degrees and baste with the melted butter that has collected at the bottom of the pan.

200

ULTIMATE ROAST CHICKEN

7. Remove the gizzards from the saucepan after they have simmered for an hour. Chill the broth so that you can easily skim the fat from the surface. (This broth will be used to make the gravy when the chicken is done roasting.)

8. Open the oven every 15 minutes and baste again. When the chicken has been in the oven for an hour, add the white wine. Continue basting every 15 minutes until the chicken has been in the oven for 1 1/2 hours (if it's stuffed, bake for 2 to 2 1/2 hours).

9. Just before taking the chicken out, put the remaining 2 tablespoons of butter into a frying pan over medium heat. Melt the butter; slowly whisk in the flour. As this mixture thickens, start adding some of the liquid from the gizzards/livers until you have a reasonable amount of gravy. When you take the chicken out, remove it from the pan and cover it with foil while it sits for a bit. Pour off as much of the fat from the pan as you can, and add whatever juices are left to your gravy. Whisk.

10. Slice the chicken and serve.

CHICKEN POTPIE

SERVES 4

INGREDIENTS
*4 cups unsalted
chicken broth
3 poached and cubed
chicken breasts
4 to 5 cups cooked cubed
vegetables (any mixture
of carrots, leeks, celery,
mushrooms, pearl
onions, zucchini, corn,
green peas)
3 tablespoons butter
4 tablespoons flour,
plus a bit extra for
rolling out dough
1 cup heavy cream
Salt and pepper to taste
9 ounces pastry dough,
store-bought or
homemade
1 egg*

1. Preheat the oven to 400 degrees.

2. Boil the chicken broth until it is reduced by half. Set aside.

3. Mix the chicken and cooked vegetables and put in a baking dish.

4. Melt the butter in a saucepan, add 4 tablespoons flour, and cook, whisking, over medium-low heat for 2 to 3 minutes. Add the broth and heavy cream. Cook, whisking, until thickened, another 3 to 4 minutes. Salt and pepper to taste and pour over the chicken and vegetables.

5. On a lightly floured surface, roll the pastry out to fit the shape of your baking dish, adding 1 1/2 inches for an overlap.

6. Whisk the egg and use some of it to brush the outside rim of the baking dish. Lay the pastry on top of the dish and crimp around the edges. Use a fork to tamp down the edges, giving it a decorative look. Brush more egg over the crust. Make a few small cuts in the crust for the steam to escape.

7. Bake for 20 minutes. Reduce the heat to 375 degrees and bake for another 15 to 20 minutes, until golden brown.

SOUTHERN FRIED CHICKEN

SERVES 4

When I was a child, a magnificent Southern cook once made fried chicken with paprika in my mother's kitchen. I spent years trying to re-create that chicken. Crisco was definitely one of her magic ingredients. After you make this dish a few times, you will be able to judge when the fat is at the right temperature (hot but not smoking), but until then, use a deep-frying thermometer. This dish goes great with mashed potatoes (see page 240). LT

INGREDIENTS

1 chicken, 3 to 4 pounds,
  cut into pieces
2 cups buttermilk
1 1/4 cups all-purpose flour,
  divided
1 1/2 teaspoons salt, divided
3/4 teaspoon pepper, divided
2 tablespoons paprika
2 cups Crisco shortening
2 cups milk

1. Coat the chicken with the buttermilk in a bowl; cover and chill for 6 to 8 hours.

2. Drain the chicken pieces, discarding the buttermilk.

3. Put 1 cup of the flour, 1 teaspoon of the salt, 1/2 teaspoon of the pepper, and all of the paprika in a big resealable plastic bag. Shake to mix. Put the chicken pieces into the bag, a couple at a time, and shake until completely covered. Let sit for 5 minutes.

4. In a cast-iron or other heavy pot, heat the shortening to 360 degrees. It should not yet be smoking. We like the sides of the pot to be high to reduce spatter.

5. Working in batches (the pieces shouldn't be touching in the skillet) and using tongs, fry the chicken slowly until it's cooked through and a deep golden brown. Cook for several minutes on each side, turning the pieces occasionally, until they have

SOUTHERN FRIED CHICKEN

cooked for 25 to 30 minutes. Drain the chicken pieces on paper towels. Keep them warm in the oven while you finish cooking the rest of the chicken.

6. When you're done frying, discard most of the fat, leaving $\frac{1}{4}$ cup of the drippings in the skillet.

7. Add $\frac{1}{4}$ cup of the flour to the drippings and cook, whisking constantly, over medium heat, until golden brown.

8. Add the milk gradually; cook, whisking constantly, for 3 to 5 minutes, or until thickened and bubbly. Stir in the remaining $\frac{1}{2}$ teaspoon salt and remaining $\frac{1}{4}$ teaspoon pepper, and serve immediately.

CHICKEN PARMESAN

SERVES 4

This is an old staple that we were always happy to eat as kids, especially if served with a side of spaghetti. Our favorite tool to flatten the raw chicken breasts is an inexpensive rubber mallet, which you can buy at any hardware or cookware store. If you want, you can flavor the bread crumbs with dried or fresh chopped herbs such as oregano, basil, or parsley. KF

INGREDIENTS
4 chicken breasts
1 large egg, beaten
2 tablespoons milk
1/2 cup bread crumbs
Salt and pepper
3 tablespoons olive oil
1 tablespoon butter
Approximately 1 1/2 cups
  Basic Tomato Sauce
  (see page 191)
1/2 cup grated
  Parmesan cheese
1/2 pound mozzarella
  cheese, cut into 4 slices

1. Preheat the oven to 400 degrees.

2. Flatten the chicken breasts to about 1/4-inch thickness. To do this, place the breasts between two pieces of plastic wrap, then pound with a wooden rolling pin or a mallet.

3. Combine the egg and milk in a shallow bowl. Mix together the bread crumbs, salt, and pepper, and spread out on a small plate. Dip the chicken in the egg mixture and then in bread crumbs, coating both sides. Set aside, in a single layer, on a plate or a piece of waxed paper.

4. Heat the oil in a frying pan; when it's hot, add the coated chicken breasts. Fry over medium heat on both sides until lightly browned, about 10 minutes total.

CHICKEN PARMESAN

5. Butter a shallow casserole dish. Add enough sauce
    to just cover the bottom, about ¹/₂ cup. Add the
    chicken breasts in a single layer and cover with a
    thin layer of sauce. Sprinkle with the Parmesan
    cheese and put one slice of mozzarella on top of
    each chicken breast.

6. Bake for 15 to 20 minutes until the cheese is
    melted and bubbling. If you wish, place under
    the broiler for a few minutes to make the cheese
    golden brown.

CHICKEN WITH MUSHROOMS

SERVES 4

This dish goes very well with Perfect Rice Pilaf (see page 238) or buttered noodles.

INGREDIENTS

6 tablespoons olive oil, divided
1 (10-ounce) container fresh button mushrooms, cleaned and sliced
1 shallot, minced
1/4 cup all-purpose flour
1/2 teaspoon salt
1/4 teaspoon freshly ground pepper
1 2 1/2- to 3-pound frying chicken, cut into pieces
1/2 cup dry white wine
1 cup chicken stock or water
1 tablespoon chopped fresh tarragon or parsley, for garnish

1. In a large frying pan, heat 3 tablespoons of the olive oil over medium heat. Add the mushrooms and shallot and cook until the mushrooms start to brown, about 7 minutes. Remove the mushroom mixture from the pan, returning the pan to the heat.

2. Put the flour, salt, and pepper into a paper or plastic bag large enough to hold half of the chicken pieces. Add half the chicken and shake to coat. Repeat until all the chicken is floured. Add the remaining 3 tablespoons of olive oil to the frying pan. Cook the chicken on all sides, in batches if necessary, until it's browned, about 15 or 20 minutes.

3. Return the mushrooms to the pan. Add the wine and the chicken stock. Turn the heat to low and cover. Cook for 20 minutes. Uncover and cook for another 10 minutes. Sprinkle with tarragon or parsley, and serve.

! Variations
- Add 1 cup of fresh or canned chopped tomatoes.
- Dried, reconstituted mushrooms can be added to give the dish an earthier flavor.

CHICKEN PAPRIKASH

SERVES 4

This is truly an international comfort food. We've found recipes for this classic dish in French, American, Australian, and German cookbooks. Serve with buttered egg noodles that have been tossed with a teaspoon of poppy or caraway seeds.

INGREDIENTS
1 cup all-purpose flour
*1 teaspoon each
    salt and pepper*
*1 (3½-pound) chicken,
    cut into 8 pieces*
1 tablespoon butter
1 tablespoon vegetable oil
1 large onion, chopped
*1 tablespoon sweet
    Hungarian paprika
    (it's worth getting the
    real thing)*
*A splash of white wine
    or white wine vinegar*
1 cup chicken broth
6 tablespoons sour cream
*Chopped fresh dill,
    for garnish (optional)*

1. Put the flour, salt, and pepper in a paper bag large enough to hold half the chicken pieces. Shake to blend.

2. Put the chicken pieces in the bag a few at a time, shake to coat, then place in a single layer on a platter or piece of waxed paper.

3. Heat the butter and oil in a skillet over medium-high heat and add the chicken. Do not crowd the pan. Cook in batches, if necessary, until brown on both sides. Remove the chicken from the pan.

4. Add the onion and sauté until softened and translucent. Add the paprika, cook for 1 minute, then add the white wine or vinegar and scrape up the brown bits from the bottom of the pan. Add the chicken broth and return the chicken to the pan.

5. Cover and simmer over low heat until the chicken is cooked through, about 35 minutes.

6. Whisk in the sour cream, taste for seasoning, and garnish with fresh dill, if you like.

CHICKEN IN A POT WITH DUMPLINGS

Like many elegant things, this simple dish is deceptive. It has some strict requirements. A large (4- to 5-pound) roasting chicken or capon is one, preferably one that has had the opportunity to run free so that it has some muscle. The other is a very light touch when it comes to the heat. The poaching liquid should never actually bubble; it should barely quiver with heat. The bird will be done in about an hour and a half when cooked in this manner. Serve with Dill Dumplings and Glazed Carrots (see page 227), or boiled egg noodles, or just bread and a salad, with coarse salt and a pot of mustard on the side.

CHICKEN IN A POT
SERVES 4 TO 5

INGREDIENTS
*1 roasting chicken or
    capon (4 to 5 pounds),
    preferably free-range
3 tablespoons butter,
    divided
1 carrot, peeled and sliced
1 small onion,
    peeled and sliced
1 small stalk celery, sliced
Salt and pepper
1 1/2 cups dry white wine
2 to 3 cups chicken broth
Fresh parsley sprigs,
    with a few leaves
    reserved for garnish
1 bay leaf*

1. Preheat the oven to 325 degrees.

2. Wash the chicken, inside and out, and pat it dry with paper towels. Remove any excess fat from the neck area. Truss the chicken or just tie the legs together so that the bird keeps its shape. Rub the bird with 2 tablespoons of the butter.

3. In a large, 6–8 quart Dutch oven or stove-to-oven casserole, sauté the carrot, onion, and celery in the remaining tablespoon of butter until soft but not brown.

4. Put the chicken in the casserole, then pour in the wine and enough chicken broth to come a third of the way up the side of the chicken. Add the parsley

CHICKEN IN A POT WITH DUMPLINGS

and bay leaf. Place a piece of waxed paper (that you have cut to fit) over the top of the chicken and bring to a simmer on the top of the stove. As soon as it begins to boil, cover the casserole with the lid and place in the middle of the preheated oven.

5. Check on the chicken in 15 or 20 minutes to make sure that the stock is not boiling and is at a gentle simmer. After 1 ¼ hours, check to see if the chicken is done. The drumsticks should be able to move in their sockets. If you are unsure, stick the tip of a paring knife in between the breast and the thigh. If juice is not pink at all, the chicken is done.

6. Remove the chicken from casserole. Taste the broth. Add salt and pepper if necessary.

7. Cut the chicken into serving pieces. (If you are making dumplings, put the chicken into a heat-proof bowl, cover with foil, and place in a 200-degree oven until you have finished the dumplings.) Serve the chicken in shallow bowls, with a ladleful of broth and vegetables (and dumplings or noodles, if desired), and a few leaves of parsley on top.

CONTINUES. . .

CHICKEN IN A POT WITH DUMPLINGS

DILL DUMPLINGS

SERVES 4 TO 5

This dumpling recipe comes from Christopher Idone's cookbook *The New Glorious American Food*. The dill is a refreshing component and typical of classic Pennsylvania Dutch cooking

INGREDIENTS
2 cups all-purpose flour
1 teaspoon baking powder
¼ teaspoon baking soda
1 teaspoon salt
*Broth from chicken
(see previous spread)*
3 tablespoons butter, melted
¾ cup buttermilk
*½ cup chopped fresh dill,
with some reserved for
garnish*

1. In a large bowl, sift together the flour, baking powder, baking soda, and salt.

2. Bring the chicken broth to a simmer.

3. Add the butter, buttermilk, and dill to the flour mixture and stir until smooth.

4. Using a soup spoon, drop large spoonfuls of the dumpling mixture into the chicken broth and cook for 5 minutes, covered. Turn the dumplings and simmer for another 5 minutes. When the dumplings are puffed and have cooked for 10 minutes, check one to see if it is cooked in the center. Continue cooking if underdone.

5. To serve, place chicken in shallow soup bowls with a ladle of broth, some vegetables, and some dumplings; sprinkle with fresh dill.

ARROZ CON POLLO

SERVES 4

A version of "chicken and rice," can be found in virtually every culture. This is Spain's interpretation, which uses the distinctive flavor of saffron. If you have never used it before, be prepared to be seduced by its exotic fragrance and gorgeous color!

INGREDIENTS
*3 cups chicken broth
(if you're using canned,
do not use low-sodium)*
*¼ teaspoon saffron,
crumbled*
*1 chicken (3 ½ to 4 pounds),
cut in pieces*
Salt and pepper
3 tablespoons olive oil
*3 cloves fresh garlic,
minced*
1 cup finely diced onion
*¾ cup diced red bell
pepper, or jarred
piquillo peppers*
1 ½ cups long-grain rice

1. In a small saucepan, heat the chicken broth to a simmer and add the saffron. Turn off the heat.

2. Season the chicken with salt and pepper. In a large heavy pot, heat the oil over a medium flame. Cook the chicken, in batches if necessary, until it's browned on all sides. Remove the chicken to a platter and set aside.

3. Add the minced garlic, onion, and red pepper to the pot and cook until tender, about 5 minutes. Add the rice and cook for a minute or two, stirring to coat with the oil in the pan.

4. Add the chicken broth. Increase the heat and bring to a boil.

5. Add the chicken. Stir, cover, reduce the heat to low, and simmer for 25 minutes or until the rice is tender.

POTATO PANCAKES

SERVES 4 TO 6

INGREDIENTS

2 medium yellow onions,
    peeled
4 medium baking potatoes,
    peeled
2 eggs
2 tablespoons matzo meal
2 teaspoons kosher salt (or
    ½ teaspoon regular,
    iodized salt)
¼ teaspoon black
    or white pepper
Vegetable oil, for frying
Sour cream or applesauce,
    for garnish

1. Grate the onions and potatoes with the fine mesh of a manual grater. Mix and pat down with paper towels to remove excess moisture.

2. In a large bowl, whisk the eggs. Add the onions, potatoes, matzo meal, salt, and pepper.

3. Put a couple of tablespoons of oil in a large skillet or griddle and heat over a medium-high flame until it is very hot (but not smoking!).

4. Drop two spoonfuls of potato mixture for each pancake into the skillet and flatten with a spatula. (You can probably fit five or six pancakes in the skillet at a time.) Cook for about 4 minutes on each side, until golden brown.

5. Remove to a platter lined with paper towels to drain. Cover with foil or put into a 200-degree oven to keep warm.

6. Serve with a tablespoon of sour cream, apple-sauce, or both.

Sides

Green Bean Casserole

SERVES 6

If we had to pick one dish from America's 1950s' table that both defines the era and has survived intact, this is it. The only difference between our recipe and the classic is that we recommend fresh, not canned, beans. But either will work.

INGREDIENTS
1 (10 ³/4-ounce) can con-
  densed cream of mush-
  room soup
³/4 cup milk
¹/8 teaspoon pepper
4 cups cooked green beans
1 ¹/2 cups canned french-fried
  onions, divided

1. Preheat the oven to 350 degrees.

2. Empty the can of condensed soup into a 1 ¹/2-quart casserole dish. Whisk in the milk and pepper. Stir in the green beans and half of the onions.

3. Bake for 30 minutes. Stir, and then sprinkle the remaining french-fried onions over the top of the casserole. Return it to the oven and bake until the topping is crisp and golden.

4. Serve immediately.

Garlic Bread
SERVES 4

They say you can't live on bread alone. But we're pretty sure *garlic* bread is the exception! It also goes perfectly with the Baked Ziti (page 190) or the Chicken Stew (page 199).

INGREDIENTS

3 cloves fresh garlic, peeled, mashed with the flat side of a chef's knife, then finely chopped
3 tablespoons butter, softened, or olive oil
Salt to taste
1 loaf French or Italian bread

1. Preheat the oven to 350 degrees. Combine the garlic, butter or olive oil, and salt in a small bowl.

2. With a sharp knife, make a 1 1/2-inch slash in the loaf of bread from one end to the other.

3. If you have a basting brush, use it to apply the garlic mixture to the inside of the bread. (If not, you can use a spoon or a small spatula—but a brush is the easiest.)

4. Place the bread on a baking sheet and bake for about 8 minutes, until heated through. Cut into slices and serve.

Roasted Winter Vegetables

SERVES 8

Every Christmas, guests come to our house and say one thing or another about brussels sprouts—"I really never eat them" or "I really don't like them." They change their minds in a big hurry after tasting these. The key is not to overcook them in the first place, and not to overcook them in the second place. In any case, they are great by themselves or with other vegetables.

INGREDIENTS

Approximately ³/4 pound
  brussels sprouts, trimmed
  (you can use fresh or frozen)
1 (1-pound) bag baby carrots
12 small potatoes (such as
  fingerlings or new potatoes)
6 small zucchini
3 tablespoons olive oil
4 onions, 1 finely diced,
  the others quartered
6 cloves garlic,
  peeled and minced
1 cup walnuts
  (whole or chopped)
Salt and pepper to taste

1. Preheat the oven to broil.

2. Steam the brussels sprouts, carrots, potatoes, and zucchini until just barely tender, about 5 minutes.

3. Rinse under cold running water, drain, and set aside.

4. Heat the olive oil in a large, deep skillet. Add the diced onions and sauté for about 5 minutes over medium heat until soft and translucent but not brown.

5. Add garlic. Sauté for another 2 minutes. Turn off the heat; add the vegetables, walnuts, and salt and pepper together in the skillet. Turn into a lightly oiled baking pan. The vegetables should be in a single layer.

6. Put the vegetables into the oven. Leave for 2 minutes, then shake the pan and put it back for another 2 minutes or until the veggies are browned and crispy on top. Watch carefully not to burn.

7. Serve warm or at room temperature.

Caramelized Onions
SERVES 6 TO 8

Here's something we didn't know until very recently: You can find peeled, frozen pearl onions at your local supermarket! They're usually sold in bags and they taste every bit as good as the ones you peel yourself, but without the tedium. You can also cook them in chicken broth instead of water, for added flavor.

INGREDIENTS
3 pints (6 cups) fresh
  or 2 (16-ounce) bags
  frozen pearl onions
6 tablespoons butter
3 tablespoons sugar
Salt and pepper to taste

1. Peel the onions and place them in a pot of salted boiling water. Simmer until tender, and drain. (For frozen onions, follow the package directions.)

2. Melt the butter in a skillet over medium heat. Add the onions, shaking the pan to coat them with butter.

3. Sprinkle with sugar, salt, and pepper, and cook until the sugar begins to caramelize. When the onions are brown, serve.

Glazed Carrots

SERVES 6

INGREDIENTS

10 to 12 medium carrots, peeled and cut into 1-inch lengths (or 2 1-pound bags of baby carrots)
4 tablespoons butter
1 1/2 tablespoons sugar
Salt and pepper to taste
1 tablespoon chopped fresh parsley

1. Set a pot of salted water on the stove to boil.

2. Cook the carrots in boiling water until tender, then drain.

3. Melt the butter in a skillet over medium heat. Add the sugar and stir until dissolved.

4. Add the carrots, tossing them in the butter until thoroughly coated. Season with salt and pepper and cook until heated through. Toss with the parsley and serve.

Southern Corn Pudding

SERVES 4 AS A SIDE DISH, OR 2 AS A MAIN COURSE

This recipe was part of most American home cooks' repertoire, up until recently. It's well worth a revival, particularly in late summer, when corn on the cob has lost its thrill. With another vegetable dish, a green salad, and a bottle of wine, it could easily become part of a vegetarian supper.

INGREDIENTS

2 eggs
2 cups whole milk (or, even better, half-and-half)
2 tablespoons melted butter
1 tablespoon sugar
1 teaspoon salt
1/8 teaspoon pepper, preferably white
2 cups fresh (or frozen) corn kernels
Freshly grated nutmeg (optional)

1. Preheat the oven to 350 degrees and put a teakettle of water on the stove to boil.

2. Break the eggs into a large bowl and whisk them together with the milk or half-and-half, butter, sugar, salt, and pepper. Stir in the corn and grate nutmeg over the top, if you're using it.

3. Pour the corn mixture into a well-buttered casserole dish, and put this dish into a larger pan. Place both into the preheated oven, and then pour boiling water into the larger pan to come halfway up the sides of the casserole dish. Bake for 35 to 40 minutes, or until set.

! Variations:
- Add 1/8 cup grated Monterey Jack or Parmesan cheese.
- Add 1/4 to 1/2 teaspoon smoked paprika or chili powder, or 1 tablespoon minced sautéed jalapeño pepper.

Sour Cream Spinach Casserole

SERVES 4

INGREDIENTS
1 (10-ounce) bag frozen chopped spinach
2 ½ cups packaged herb croutons
1 ¼ cups sour cream
1 packet dried onion soup mix
2 tablespoons melted butter

1. Put the frozen spinach in a fine strainer over a bowl to drain and let it defrost. When it's defrosted, press out the excess liquid with the back of a spoon.

2. Preheat the oven to 350 degrees.

3. Crush the croutons in a plastic bag with a rolling pin (or wine bottle) until they are close to the consistency of bread crumbs, but not totally pulverized.

4. Combine the spinach, sour cream, and onion soup mix in a large bowl, then spread the mixture evenly in a 1 ½-quart casserole dish.

5. Sprinkle the crushed croutons evenly over the surface, then drizzle with butter.

6. Cover with a lid (or aluminum foil) and bake for 30 minutes, until heated through. Remove the lid or foil and continue baking until the top is a light golden brown, about 10 minutes.

First we eat, then we do everything else.

M. F. K. Fisher

Collard Greens

SERVES 6 TO 8

This is a great Southern dish. Dark, leafy greens are very good for you, and this is a delicious way to prepare them—especially when served with barbecued ribs or chicken. A little Tabasco won't hurt, either!

INGREDIENTS

3/4 pound slab bacon, cut into large cubes
4 pounds well-washed collard greens, stalks removed
3 dried red chili peppers, or 1 teaspoon crushed red pepper
1 tablespoon sugar
2 tablespoons cider vinegar
Pickapeppa Sauce (or other bottled hot sauce) to taste
Salt and freshly ground pepper to taste

1. Fry the bacon in a large pot. Then add the collard greens, chili peppers, and 3 quarts water. Simmer for about 2 hours, or until tender. Drain in a colander.

2. Return the greens to the pot and add the sugar, cider vinegar, Pickapeppa Sauce, and salt and pepper. Mix until blended, and serve.

Creamed Spinach

SERVES 6

It took us many years to fall in love with spinach, despite Popeye, but once we did, we fell in love wholeheartedly. Creamed spinach, steamed spinach, spinach salad, any and all spinach dishes—we now love them all. But creamed spinach is particularly comforting and perfect with fish, chicken, or beef.

INGREDIENTS
4 tablespoons butter
1 cup minced onions
    (1 large or 2 medium)
3 (10-ounce) bags fresh
    spinach, well washed
    (baby spinach is the best)
1 cup heavy cream
Salt and freshly
    ground pepper to taste
1/2 cup grated Parmesan
    cheese (optional)

1. Melt the butter in a small sauté pan over medium heat. Add the onions and cook slowly until they are translucent and soft. Set aside.

2. Put a large sauté pan with a lid over medium heat. When it is hot, start adding the freshly washed spinach in batches. Put in as much spinach as the pan can hold, and put on the lid. (The water clinging to the leaves will create steam, to cook the spinach.) As it wilts, add more, until all the spinach is cooked but remains bright green.

3. Pour out excess liquid. Add the onions, cream, salt, and pepper.

4. Put a third of this mixture into a blender and process until you are happy with the consistency. (If you don't want it to be a puree, use a food processor instead, and gently pulse it until the spinach has been chopped, rather than pureed.) Transfer to a serving bowl. Follow the same steps with the remaining two thirds.

5. Taste, adjust the seasonings, and sprinkle cheese on top if you wish. Serve immediately.

Wild Rice Casserole

SERVES 8 TO 10 AS A SIDE DISH

It wouldn't be a book on comfort food without casseroles. This one comes from the Midwest. Our friend's aunt serves it for Sunday brunch every week (she adds in a pound of crumbled sausage to make it more of a main course). This vegetarian version is a perfect side dish.

INGREDIENTS

2 cups wild rice
chicken broth (approximately 4-8 cups depending on brand of rice)
1 (10-ounce) package fresh button mushrooms, sliced (about 3 cups)
1 medium onion, chopped
2 tablespoons olive oil
2 (10 3/4-ounce) cans cream of mushroom soup
1 teaspoon salt
1/2 teaspoon ground pepper
2/3 cup seasoned bread crumbs

1. Rinse the rice well with warm water to remove any sand and grit. Prepare rice according to instructions on package, but substitute chicken broth for water. (It should simmer, covered, for approximately 45 minutes.)

2. While the rice cooks, sauté the mushrooms and onion in the olive oil until the onion is translucent.

3. Preheat the oven to 350 degrees.

4. When the rice is cooked, drain it , and then combine with the onion–mushroom mixture, cream of mushroom soup, salt, and pepper.

5. Spoon the mixture into a buttered 9- by 13-inch pan or a 3 1/2-quart casserole dish. Sprinkle with the seasoned bread crumbs.

6. Cover with foil and bake for 30 minutes, and then remove the foil and bake for another 30 minutes.

7. Serve warm. (This can also be made the day before and reheated.)

Rice Pilaf

SERVES 2 TO 4

This recipe is so simple, and works so well, that the myth of rice being "tricky" to make will forever be dispelled from your list of cooking phobias.

INGREDIENTS
2 tablespoon butter
2 tablespoons chopped onions, shallots, or scallions
¼ cup dry spaghetti or linguine, broken into small pieces
1 cup long-grain rice (preferably Carolina brand)
2 cups canned chicken broth

1. Melt the butter over medium heat in a 1 ½-quart saucepan.

2. Add the onions and cook for a minute or two, until soft and translucent. Add the pieces of spaghetti and the rice; sauté until the rice becomes opaque and white and the pasta starts to brown.

3. Add the chicken broth, bring to a boil, and then turn the heat to low and cover the pot tightly. Check after 15 minutes; if the broth isn't entirely absorbed, cook for another few minutes. Turn off the heat and let the pilaf sit, covered for 5 minutes. Toss the pilaf with a fork and cover once more. The pilaf can sit for 10 to 15 minutes before serving.

! Variations:
· Add a large pinch of saffron to the pot when you add the chicken stock.
· Add some toasted pine nuts and chopped fresh parsley or cilantro after the rice has been cooked.

Turkey Stuffing
WILL STUFF A 14- TO 18-POUND BIRD

INGREDIENTS
1 onion, minced
*½ cup chopped chestnuts
(vacuum-packed or
canned are fine)*
½ cup chopped celery
*½ cup chopped mushrooms
of your choice*
2 tablespoons olive oil
*1 large bag (14 ounces)
Pepperidge Farm Country
Style or Herb Seasoned
Stuffing mix*
*1 ¼ cup minced fresh
Italian parsley*
*1 tablespoon chopped
fresh rosemary*
*1 tablespoon chopped
fresh thyme*
*1 tablespoon chopped
fresh sage*
*1 cup canned chicken broth
(if cooking outside the bird)*

1. Sauté the onions, chestnuts, celery, and mushrooms in the olive oil until softened and slightly browned.

2. Prepare the stuffing according to package instructions. Stir in the onion mixture along with the herbs.

3. If you are stuffing a turkey, stuff and bake as directed. If not, spoon stuffing into 2 buttered loaf pans and bake for 45 minutes at 350 degrees. Baste occasionally with chicken broth.

4. Serve warm.

Cranberry Sauce
SERVES 8

This is the easiest recipe in the world. It's even on the bag. But it makes the greatest cranberry sauce you'll ever have, free of orange rind and all that other fussy stuff some people like to add in. This is pure cranberry, and we defy you to bring it to Thanksgiving dinner and not get raves!

INGREDIENTS
*1 (12-ounce) bag fresh
   or frozen cranberries*
1 cup sugar

1. Combine all the ingredients in a pot with one cup of water. Cook for about 15 minutes, or until the cranberries have burst.

2. Cool completely before serving. That's it!

Mashed Potatoes
SERVES 4 TO 6

When it comes to mashed potatoes, we are purists. We'll leave the herbs, garlic, sour cream, parmesan cheese, and all the other popular add-ins for the restaurant chefs. At our home, it's just butter, cream, salt, pepper, and potatoes.
Irresistable.

INGREDIENTS
*6 baking potatoes
    (preferably russets),
    peeled and halved*
*1 stick (8 tablespoons) butter,
    cut into pieces*
1/4 cup heavy cream
1/2 cup milk
*Salt and freshly
    ground pepper to taste*

1. Place the potatoes in enough lightly salted cold
   water to cover them. Bring to a boil, turn down the
   heat and simmer for approximately 15-20 minutes,
   or until soft. Drain and return to the pot.

2. Add butter and mash the potatoes until the butter
   has melted. Place over medium heat and gradually
   pour in cream and milk, stirring with a wooden
   spoon. Mix until smooth and creamy.

3. Stir in seasonings, and serve.

Small cheer and great
welcome makes a merry feast.

William Shakespeare

Maple Syrup Sweet Potatoes

SERVES 4

We used to buy our mashed sweet potatoes for Thanksgiving from Yura's, a marvelous New York caterer. But when we moved our holiday celebrations to California, we had to figure out how to replicate it at home. This is it.

INGREDIENTS

4 sweet potatoes (or yams), peeled and quartered
4 tablespoons butter
4 tablespoons heavy cream
8 tablespoons maple syrup
Nutmeg, cinnamon, salt, and freshly ground pepper to taste

1. Cover the potatoes in lightly salted cold water and cook over high heat. Bring to a boil, then turn the heat down and simmer until done, approximately 20 minutes.

2. Drain the potatoes and return them to the pot.

3. Mash the potatoes, adding butter until completely melted. Over medium heat and stirring with a wooden spoon, gradually pour in the cream, and finally, the maple syrup. Mix until the potatoes are smooth and creamy.

4. Add seasonings to taste.

Smashed Red-Skinned Potatoes

SERVES 4 TO 6

This is an easier, lower fat version of the classic mashed potatoes.
The potatoes don't need to be peeled, and there's no dairy. The
red—or "bliss"—potatoes have a naturally creamy texture that is
enhanced by the olive oil. And you can throw whatever seasonings in
that you like: roasted garlic, flavored oils, etc.

INGREDIENTS

2 pounds small red potatoes
1/2 teaspoon salt,
  plus more to taste
3 to 4 tablespoons olive oil
2 tablespoons chopped
  fresh parsley
Pepper

1. Place the potatoes in a large pot and cover
   with cold water by 2 inches. Bring to a boil, turn
   down the heat, and simmer until the potatoes are
   slightly overcooked (their skins will crack and the
   potatoes will split easily when stabbed with a
   fork)—approximately 20 minutes.

2. Drain the potatoes and add the olive oil to the pot.
   Mash with a potato masher. Add the parsley and
   salt and pepper to taste. For a creamier texture,
   add a little more oil.

! Variation: Add a clove or two of peeled garlic to the potatoes as they are boiling.
The garlic will become soft and can be mashed along with the potatoes.

Twice Baked Potatoes
SERVES 8

INGREDIENTS
*8 medium Idaho
    or russet potatoes
1 pound fresh mushrooms,
    cleaned and sliced
3 tablespoons olive oil
Salt and pepper
1 cup whole milk
6 tablespoons butter, divided
3 tablespoons chopped
    fresh parsley
Parmesan cheese,
    grated (optional)*

1. Preheat the oven to 400 degrees. Put one rack in the middle of the oven, and another rack right below it.

2. Prick the potatoes with a fork and place them on the middle rack. Bake them for about an hour.

3. While the potatoes are baking, put the sliced mushrooms on a sheet pan and toss them with the olive oil, salt, and pepper. Cover the pan with foil and place it on the rack beneath the potatoes. Bake for 15 minutes. Remove the foil and roast for another 15 or 20 minutes.

4. When the potatoes offer no resistance when pierced with a fork or toothpick, remove them from the oven.

5. When the potatoes are cool enough to handle, slash the top of each one lengthwise. Scoop its flesh into a bowl, leaving a shell about 1/4 inch thick.

6. Meanwhile, heat the milk and 3 tablespoons of the butter in a small saucepan (or microwave) until the butter is melted. Add this to the potatoes and mash until the liquid is incorporated and the potatoes are smooth. Fold the roasted mushrooms and the

Twice Baked Potatoes

chopped parsley into the mashed-potato mixture. Add salt and pepper to taste.

7. Place the potato shells on a baking sheet and brush their insides with the remaining melted butter. Season with salt. Return to the oven. Bake for about 15 minutes.

8. Remove the baked shells and fill them with the mashed potato mixture. Sprinkle lightly with grated Parmesan cheese. At this point, the potatoes can be refrigerated until you are ready to serve.

9. To serve, bake the potatoes in a 400-degree oven for 15 or 20 minutes, until thoroughly heated.

! **Variation—Baked Potatoes with Broccoli and Cheddar:** Omit the mushrooms and Parmesan. While the potatoes are baking, steam florets from two heads of broccoli until just tender. Plunge into ice water (to stop the cooking and maintain the fresh, green color) and drain. Grate 1 1/2 cups cheddar cheese. In step 8, top the mashed potato mixture with some of the broccoli and the cheddar. Bake until the cheese has melted and the potato is heated through.

Scalloped Potatoes

SERVES 6

It seems like every culture has a version of this dish. The French refer to it as Gratin de Pommes de Terre. We call it Scalloped Potatoes. Either way, it's real comfort food.

INGREDIENTS

1 tablespoon butter
2 pounds starchy potatoes,
  such as russet or Yukon
  Gold, peeled and sliced
  very thin (¹/8 to ¹/16 inch
  thick), about 6 medium-
  sized potatoes
2 onions,
  peeled and sliced thin
2 cloves garlic, peeled,
  flattened and minced
Salt and pepper
1 ¹/2 cups half-and-half
¹/2 cup heavy cream

1. Preheat the oven to 325 degrees. Use butter to grease a shallow 9- by 9-inch or 8- by 10-inch baking dish.

2. Layer the potatoes and onions in the baking dish with the garlic, salt, and pepper.

3. Pour half-and-half over the potatoes until they are barely covered. Bake for 45 minutes.

4. Drizzle heavy cream over the top and continue to bake for another 45 minutes or until golden brown. Serve warm.

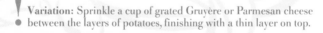

Variation: Sprinkle a cup of grated Gruyère or Parmesan cheese between the layers of potatoes, finishing with a thin layer on top.

Perfect Potato Salad

SERVES 4 TO 6

INGREDIENTS

*2 pounds potatoes
 (preferably a low-starch
 variety such as Yellow
 Finn, red-skinned,
 or white potatoes)*
1 tablespoon salt
1/3 cup chicken stock
2 tablespoons cider vinegar
1 cup mayonnaise
2 tablespoons Dijon mustard
*2/3 cup finely
 chopped scallions*
1/2 cup finely chopped celery
*3 tablespoons finely chopped
 fresh chives or Italian
 parsley*
Salt and pepper to taste

1. Place the unpeeled potatoes in a pot and cover with cold water. Add a tablespoon of salt, bring to a boil, and cook until tender but not mushy, about 15 minutes.

2. While the potatoes are cooking, mix the chicken stock and vinegar together in a small bowl. In a separate bowl, mix the mayonnaise, Dijon mustard, scallions, celery, and chives or parsley.

3. When the potatoes are tender, drain them. Cut them into halves, quarters, or whatever size you prefer.

4. Pour the chicken stock mixture over the potatoes, toss gently, and let the potatoes absorb the liquid.

5. Gently toss the potatoes with the mayonnaise mixture, season to taste with salt and pepper, and toss again.

6. This salad tastes best if it is not refrigerated, and served an hour or so after being made. If you want to make it well ahead of time, then cover it and refrigerate, but let it stand at room temperature for 20 minutes before serving.

 Variation: For a lighter potato salad, you can replace mayonnaise with 1 cup chicken stock.

Down Home Potato Chips

SERVES 4 TO 6

INGREDIENTS

2 medium-size Idaho
   potatoes, scrubbed
2 tablespoons crumbled
   herbs or spices, such as
   dill, rosemary, dried onion
   flakes, or chili powder
1/2 teaspoon garlic salt
1/4 teaspoon pepper
Nonstick cooking spray
1 tablespoon olive oil

1. Preheat the oven to 450 degrees.

2. Slice the potatoes very thin and pat dry with paper towels.

3. In a small bowl, combine the herbs, garlic salt, and pepper. Set aside.

4. Coat a baking sheet with nonstick cooking spray and arrange the potato slices in a single layer on the sheet.

5. Spray the potato slices with more cooking spray. Bake for 10 minutes.

6. Turn the slices over and brush with the olive oil. Sprinkle the herb mixture evenly onto the slices. Bake for 5 to 10 minutes longer, or until the chips are golden brown.

7. Cool on the baking sheet before serving.

Cheesy Potato Skins

MAKES 32 SKINS

INGREDIENTS

2 medium-size baking
   potatoes
2 tablespoons butter, softened
1 cup grated cheddar cheese
4 slices bacon,
   cooked and crumbled
1/4 cup sour cream
2 tablespoons chopped
   black olives
2 tablespoons finely chopped
   chives (optional)

1. Preheat the oven to 425 degrees.

2. Scrub the potatoes well and pierce them with a fork.
   Bake on the bottom rack of the oven for 1 hour, or
   until tender when tested with a fork. Let them cool.

3. Cut the potatoes in half lengthwise. With a large
   spoon, scoop out the center of each potato, leaving
   a shell thickness of about 1/2 inch. (Store the
   scooped-out potato in a container for another use.)

4. Quarter the potato halves. Then cut each quarter
   in half to create 32 triangular wedges. Arrange
   the potato skins on a foil- or parchment-lined
   cookie sheet.

5. Brush the insides of the potato skins with the butter and bake for 8 to 12 minutes, or until golden
   and crispy. Remove from the oven.

6. Sprinkle the potato skins with cheese and bake for
   another 5 minutes, or until the cheese melts.

7. Sprinkle crumbled bacon atop each skin. Add a
   dollop of sour cream, and top with olives and
   chives. Serve while hot.

Un-French Fries

SERVES 4

These are a perfect accompaniment to our burgers on page 85. They're much healthier than what you might get at a fast-food restaurant. But they will satisfy the craving!

INGREDIENTS:
1 ½ pounds baking potatoes (3 large), peeled (or not) and cut into ¼-inch-square sticks
1 tablespoon grated Parmesan cheese
1 tablespoon olive or other vegetable oil
¼ teaspoon each salt, garlic powder, paprika, and pepper

1. Preheat the oven to 450 degrees.

2. Combine all the ingredients in a bowl. Mix thoroughly, then transfer to an ungreased baking sheet. Spread out into a single layer.

3. Bake for 25 minutes, or until the potatoes are tender and brown.

Beverages

Hot Chocolate with Whipped Cream

SERVES 2

Most people think hot chocolate is easy, but there is a big difference between a good cup of hot chocolate and a great one. Our dad believed the secret is to use real chocolate instead of cocoa and to whip the hot chocolate in the pot as it heated on the stove. And he always made his own whipped cream. KF

Hot Chocolate

INGREDIENTS
2 cups milk
1 cup cream
4 ounces bittersweet choco-
*   late, the best available*
2 tablespoons sugar

1. Combine the milk, cream, chocolate, and sugar in a saucepan and heat over a low flame, stirring constantly with an eggbeater or whisk.

2. When the mixture is smooth and just starting to bubble, remove it from the heat and pour into two mugs. Serve with cinnamon sticks, peppermint sticks, fresh whipped cream (recipe follows), or marshmallows.

Whipped Cream

INGREDIENTS
1/2 pint whipping cream
1 teaspoon vanilla or pepper-
*   mint extract*
1 teaspoon white sugar

1. Combine the ingredients in a mixing bowl.

2. Whip with an electric mixer or by hand until stiff peaks form.

3. Spoon the whipped cream onto the steaming hot chocolate. Or it can be covered and refrigerated for several hours.

Variations: Add 1 tablespoon of peppermint schnapps to each cup and serve with peppermint whipped cream for a more adult version of this classic.

If you are not feeling well, if you have not slept, chocolate will revive you. But you have no chocolate! I think of that again and again! My dear, how will you ever manage?

Marquise de Sévigné

Ice Cream Soda

SERVES 1

INGREDIENTS
*2 to 3 tablespoons chocolate
    or strawberry syrup
Chilled soda water
2 scoops ice cream
1 to 2 spoonfuls
    whipped cream (optional)*

1. Pour the syrup into an 8-ounce soda glass and add soda water. Stir well until the mixture is foaming at the top.

2. Add the ice cream and top with whipped cream, if desired.

3. Serve immediately with a straw and a long spoon.

! **Variation—Root Beer Float:** Just substitute the syrup and soda water for a chilled bottle of old-fashioned root beer!

Egg Cream

SERVES 1

An egg cream is a New York specialty that has been around since the 1930s. Contrary to what the name suggests, there is no egg in an egg cream. When made properly, it has a foamy froth on top that resembles beaten egg whites or the foam from a cappuccino.

INGREDIENTS
*2 tablespoons
    chocolate syrup
6 ounces whole milk, chilled
6 ounces soda water, chilled*

1. Mix the syrup and milk in a large glass. Add the soda water slowly. Then, using a long spoon, stir quickly to create a head of foam.

2. Serve immediately with a straw.

Vanilla Milkshake

SERVES 1

It is no exaggeration to say that I grew up drinking five (or more) milkshakes a week. My father was a famed milkshake master. A Black & White (my favorite) was made simply with vanilla Häagen Dazs® ice cream, whole milk, and a generous pour of Hershey's chocolate syrup. All the fixings went into a used tin coffee can (Chock Full O' Nuts), ready to be transformed. We didn't have an electric blender, just a hand crank mixer that always left my little girl arm weak and aching after just a few minutes of exertion. But my father always made it look like a breeze, and in a matter of minutes, the contents of the can would turn into a frothy velvety liquid. The secret to its airy perfection, he counseled, was in keeping a constant steady speed. "*Never* stop," he warned me once. "Not even to scratch an itch." The shake was declared ready only when the creamy bubbles had risen so high in the can they threatened to spill over the edge. Swiftly, my father reached for a waiting empty fountain glass with "Coca Cola" stenciled on the side, and filled it to the brim. That first taste was so delicious, I remember wishing I'd never reach the the bottom of the glass. And there always seemed to be a sip or two left over in the can—a small reward for the milkshake maker himself. KF

INGREDIENTS
*3 to 4 scoops vanilla
    ice cream*
1/2 cup milk
1/4 cup vanilla syrup
1/2 teaspoon vanilla extract

1. Pour all the ingredients into a blender and blend until smooth. The longer you blend the shake, the thinner it will become, so blend to your desired consistency.

2. Pour into two large glasses—topping each, if you wish, with whipped cream and a maraschino cherry. Serve immediately with a straw.

Variations:
- **Chocolate:** Substitute chocolate ice cream and chocolate syrup.
- **Black-and-white:** Use chocolate syrup with the vanilla ice cream.
- **Strawberry:** Use strawberry syrup and ice cream.
- **Chocolate malt:** Follow the instructions for a chocolate shake, but before blending add a heaping scoop of malted-milk powder.

Sherbet Fizz

SERVES 6

This old-fashioned favorite is perfect for a pool party—or any hot afternoon!

INGREDIENTS
8 ounces orange juice
1 (20-ounce) can chunk
  pineapple, with juice
16 ounces (2 cups)
  lemon sherbet
    12 ounces ginger ale
    8 strawberries, for
    garnish

1. Combine the orange juice, pineapple, and sherbet in a blender, and whir until smooth. Pour into a large pitcher.

2. Add the ginger ale to the pitcher and stir with a wooden spoon.

3. To make strawberry garnishes, first remove the stem from each strawberry. Next, make 4 to 6 deep cuts about 1/2 inch from the top, and twist the berry slightly so that it spreads out like a fan. Place a strawberry fan on top of each drink or on the rim of the glass and serve.

Shirley Temple

SERVES 1

This is a classic kids' favorite, but isn't that why we love it so much as adults? (When served to a boy it was called a Roy Rogers.) Try one the next time you need cheering up. It works, we promise. And don't forget the cherry.

INGREDIENTS
Ice cubes
1 tablespoon
  maraschino cherry syrup
1 to 2 cups ginger ale
1 maraschino cherry

1. Fill an 8-ounce soda glass with ice cubes. Add the syrup and ginger ale, and stir.

2. Garnish with the cherry and serve immediately.

Homemade Root Beer

SERVES 10 TO 12

INGREDIENTS
1 teaspoon dry yeast
2 cups sugar
4 teaspoons root beer extract

1. In a small bowl, dissolve the yeast in $1/2$ cup warm water.

2. In a large bowl, dissolve the sugar in 4 cups of hot water.

3. In a 1-gallon jar, mix the contents of both bowls, and add the root beer extract.

4. Fill the jar with warm water, stir, and cover. Leave it in a warm spot for 4 hours, then leave it covered overnight.

5. Chill the root beer and serve.

Fresh Ginger Ale

SERVES 10 TO 12

A glass of cold ginger ale is invigorating when you're hot and tired. But there's also a good reason that your mother brought you flat ginger ale when you had a stomachache. Ginger has been used in China as a natural anti-nausea medication for 2,500 years. This recipe is easy, and the base keeps for a couple of weeks in the refrigerator.

INGREDIENTS
2 cups fresh gingerroot,
  peeled and chopped
3 strips lemon peel
2 cups sugar
Ice cubes, for serving
Seltzer, for serving

1. Combine the ginger, lemon peel, and sugar with 4 cups of water in a 3- to 4-quart saucepan. Bring to a boil over high heat, then simmer for 20 minutes. Strain the syrup and chill.

2. To serve, put ice cubes in a tall glass and add $1/4$ cup ginger syrup. Add seltzer to taste.

263

Thank God for tea!
What would the
world do without tea!
How did it exist?
I am glad I was not
born before tea.

William Gladstone

A Perfect Pot of Tea

SERVES 6

When we started working on this book, there were a few recipes that, to us, literally defined "comfort food." Tea may not technically be a food, but it was still in the top five. When we need comfort, want to relax, or just feel cozy, the first thing we have always done is put on the kettle. We've spent hundreds of hours sitting around the kitchen counter drinking tea and sharing our lives; complaining, celebrating, commiserating. And as any true tea drinker will tell you, a pot of fresh-brewed loose tea is infinitely better than the kind made with the bagged variety. For a real treat, make yourself some scones or popovers to go along with it and curl up with a good book!

INGREDIENTS
4 teaspoons tea leaves

1. Put the tea leaves in a large teapot. In a kettle, bring 5 cups of water just to a rolling boil; remove from the heat. Pour the water into the teapot and allow the tea leaves to steep for exactly 4 minutes.

2. Immediately pour the tea through a strainer into six teacups. You can also omit the strainer and allow the tea leaves to settle into each cup.

3. Serve immediately with your choice of lemon or cream, honey, or sugar.

Coffee Drinks

These are truly decadent treats. They will warm you from the inside out. And they are filling enough to be breakfast all by themselves, or dessert. Use your favorite coffee brand—ours is Peet's, which can be ordered online. It's always better to grind your own beans, right before you brew, if you can. And store unused coffee in the freezer to keep it fresher, longer.

Café au Lait • Caffe con Leche

INGREDIENTS
1 part hot,
   freshly brewed coffee
1 part hot milk
   (do not allow to boil)

Combine and sweeten to taste.

Mocha Coffee

INGREDIENTS
3 tablespoons
   chocolate syrup
Dash of cinnamon
1 cup hot,
   freshly brewed coffee
Whipped cream

Pour the syrup and cinnamon into the coffee, stir well, and top with whipped cream.

Hot Toddy
SERVES 1

A hot toddy supposedly helps cure colds. . . and even if it doesn't, it will warm you up!

INGREDIENTS
1 teaspoon honey
2 shots brandy
A squeeze and a slice of lemon
Hot tea

Add the honey, brandy, and lemon to a cup of freshly brewed tea. Relax and enjoy.

Hot Buttered Rum
SERVES 1

INGREDIENTS
Angostura bitters
3 ounces dark rum
1 teaspoon butter
3 or 4 whole cloves

1. Put a kettle of water on the stove and bring to a boil.
2. Put a few dashes of Angostura bitters into a mug along with the rum, butter, and whole cloves.
3. Add boiling water to fill the mug, then let the mixture steep a few moments. Remove the cloves before serving.

Bloody Mary Mix

SERVES 10

This recipe for Bloody Mary Mix is adapted from the restaurant *The Hungry Cat* in Hollywood, and makes enough for 10 drinks. Balance is the key here. It's easy to make your own tomato juice: Just whirl some super-ripe tomatoes in a blender and strain out the seeds and skins.

INGREDIENTS

8 large pimiento-stuffed green olives
2 red jalapeño peppers, grilled over gas flame and peeled
Juice of 2 lemons
Juice of 2 limes
3 tablespoons Worcestershire sauce
1 heaping tablespoon prepared horseradish
1/2 teaspoon freshly ground black pepper
8 dashes Tabasco
4 cups tomato juice, preferably homemade
Vodka, for serving
Kosher salt, for serving

1. Put the olives, jalapeños, lemon and lime juice, Worcestershire, horseradish, black pepper, and Tabasco into a blender, and puree.

2. Add this blender mixture to the tomato juice.

3. To make one serving, fill a 9-ounce glass with ice. Add 4 ounces Bloody Mary Mix plus 1 1/2 ounces vodka, and stir until chilled. Sprinkle with a little kosher salt and serve.

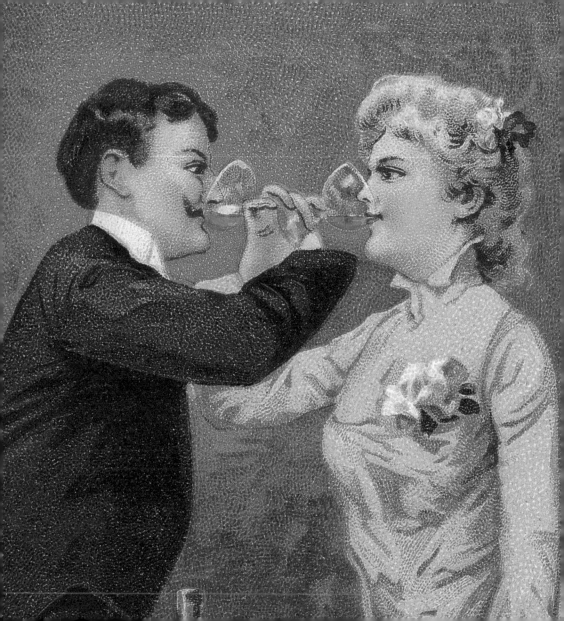

Mulled Apple Cider

SERVES 4

We love to make this in the fall when we entertain, no matter what the meal. It fills the house with the most welcoming smells, and everyone loves it. You can add a shot of brandy to each cup if you want to make it more sophisticated. It will keep in the fridge for several days.

INGREDIENTS

*1 quart (4 cups) apple juice
    or apple cider
Peel from ½ orange
1 1-inch slice peeled fresh
    gingerroot
1 teaspoon whole allspice
6 cinnamon sticks
Additional cinnamon sticks,
    1 per cup (kids love to try
    to use them as straws!)*

1. Put the juice or cider in a large saucepan over the lowest heat.

2. Wrap up the remaining ingredients in a big piece of cheesecloth. Put it into the pot; or put the ingredients into a strainer that hooks over the pot. Simmer over the lowest heat for 1 ½ to 2 hours.

3. Throw away the spices and pour the cider into 4 mugs, adding a cinnamon stick to each.

Holiday Eggnog

SERVES 12

INGREDIENTS

6 organic eggs, separated
*1 3/4 cups superfine
    granulated sugar, divided*
4 cups (1 quart) half-and-half
1/2 cup rum
1 cup brandy
1 cup bourbon
1 tablespoon vanilla extract
3 cups heavy cream
1 tablespoon ground nutmeg

1. Using an electric mixer, beat the egg yolks with 1/2 cup of the sugar until foamy and thickened, then add the half-and-half, rum, brandy, bourbon, and vanilla.

2. Beat the egg whites until they start to become thick and foamy, then add 3/4 cup of the sugar in a stream; continue beating until the whites form soft, glossy peaks.

3. In a separate bowl, beat the heavy cream with the remaining 1/2 cup sugar until thick but not stiff.

4. Fold the whipped egg whites and whipped heavy cream into the egg-yolk mixture. Chill.

5. Sprinkle with nutmeg. Serve from a punch bowl with a ladle.

*✳ Note:** If you are concerned about the health risks associated with the consumption of raw eggs, you should avoid this recipe.

Scandinavian Glogg

SERVES 8 TO 14

The house will smell fabulous after you make this glogg, and the fruit compotes—
which you'll be eating for days afterward—are spectacular.

INGREDIENTS
1 (2-quart) bottle ruby port
1 cup raisins
1 cup whole blanched
  almonds
8 cardamom pods
5 whole cloves
3 cinnamon sticks
Zest of 1 lemon, cut into strips
Zest of 1 navel orange,
  cut into strips
2 cups mixed dried apricots,
  apples, and seedless prunes
1 (2-quart) bottle dry red
  wine (an inexpensive
  bottle will do)
Aquavit (to taste)

1. Pour the port into a nonaluminum saucepan with
    the raisins and almonds. Wrap the spices, zests,
    and dried fruits together in a large piece of cheese-
    cloth or muslin and add this to the pot. (You can
    alter quantities to suit your taste.)

2. Simmer over low heat for 1 hour.

3. Turn off the heat, cover the pan, and let the glogg
    steep for a day.

4. To serve: Remove the cheesecloth bag or strainer
    (save the fruits for a delicious compote that can be
    served with whipped cream or over ice
    cream as a dessert!) and add the dry red
    wine to the pot.

5. Heat the mixture over a low
    flame until it's very hot. Pour
    into glasses, add some
    raisins and almonds
    from the pot, and top
    with a tablespoon of
    aquavit.

277

Old-Fashioned Lemonade

SERVES 6 TO 8

To turn this into pink lemonade, just add a touch of cranberry juice.

INGREDIENTS

2 cups sugar
Water
1 1/2 cups freshly squeezed
   lemon juice (about 6
   large lemons)
2 lemons, thinly sliced,
   for serving
3 or 4 sprigs fresh mint
   leaves, for serving

1. Combine the sugar with 1 cup water in a medium saucepan. Boil until the sugar is dissolved, and then remove from the heat.

2. In a large pitcher, combine the sugar syrup, lemon juice, and 8 cups cold water.

3. Serve the lemonade over ice, garnished with lemon slices and mint.

Iced Sun Tea

SERVES 6

Is there anything better on a hot summer afternoon? Set it out in the morning to brew, and enjoy in the shade, come teatime.

INGREDIENTS

4 tea bags
2 lemons, thinly sliced and
   halved, for serving
Sugar, for serving

1. Combine 8 cups of cold water and the tea bags in a large pitcher. Place in a sunny spot and let the mixture sit for up to 6 hours.

2. Remove the tea from the sun, stir well, and remove the tea bags. Serve over ice with lemon slices to garnish. Sweeten to taste.

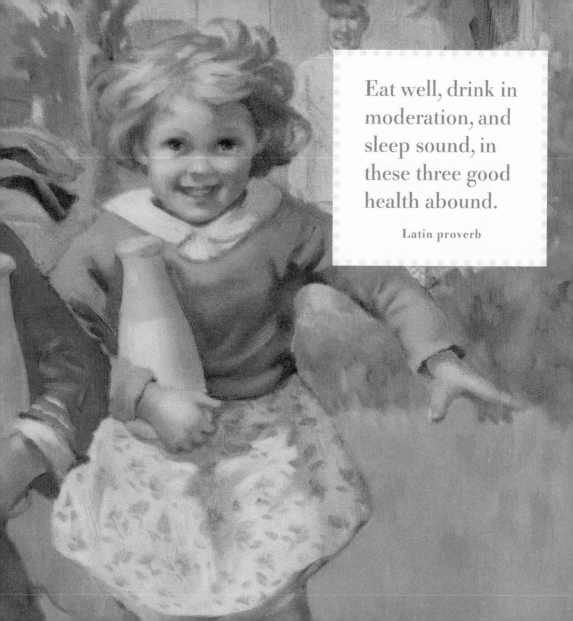

Eat well, drink in moderation, and sleep sound, in these three good health abound.

Latin proverb

desserts

pecan pie

SERVES 8 TO 10

INGREDIENTS
For the pastry:
12 tablespoons (1 1/2 sticks;
3/4 cup) unsalted butter
3 cups all-purpose flour
3 tablespoons sugar
2 egg yolks, lightly beaten
About 1/4 cup ice water

For the filling:
5 whole eggs
1 egg yolk
1 cup packed
light brown sugar
2 tablespoons melted butter
2 teaspoons vanilla extract
2 to 3 tablespoons bourbon
3 cups pecan pieces,
lightly toasted

1. Make the pastry: In a mixing bowl, cut the butter into the flour until it reaches the consistency of fine meal.

2. Sprinkle on the sugar and add the beaten egg yolks and ice water. Lightly blend together. Form the dough into a ball, wrap it in waxed paper, and chill for at least 20 minutes.

3. Preheat the oven to 350 degrees.

4. Prepare the filling: In a bowl, mix together all the filling ingredients except the pecans and blend well.

5. Assemble the pie: Roll out the pastry on a lightly floured surface and fit it into a 9-inch pie pan. Spread the pecan pieces evenly over the pie shell. Pour the filling mixture over the nuts. Bake for 1 hour, or until golden brown.

6. Cool to room temperature before serving.

apple crumb pie

SERVES 6 TO 8

This is so classic. Add a scoop of vanilla ice cream and it's heaven. The store-bought piecrust is the secret—it allows you to enjoy baking without all the work.

INGREDIENTS

For the filling:
3/4 cup sugar
3 tablespoons
  all-purpose flour
1 tablespoon ground cinnamon
1/4 teaspoon
  ground nutmeg
1/8 teaspoon salt
Juice of 1 lemon
6 apples, peeled, cored,
  and sliced thin
1 frozen piecrust

For the topping:
3/4 cup all-purpose flour
1/2 cup packed brown sugar
8 tablespoons (1 stick)
  unsalted butter, softened
Pinch of salt
1 tablespoon ground cinnamon
1/4 teaspoon ground nutmeg

1. Preheat the oven to 425 degrees.

2. In a bowl, mix the sugar, flour, cinnamon, nutmeg, salt, and lemon juice. Add the apples and toss to coat thoroughly.

3. Fill the piecrust with the apple mixture, mounding it slightly.

4. In a bowl, combine the ingredients for the topping. Crumble with your hands, then sprinkle over the apple mixture.

5. Bake until golden brown, approximately 40 minutes.

pumpkin pie

SERVES 8 TO 10

We're amazed more people don't make pumpkin pie year-round—it's one of the most comforting desserts we know. Make your own crust, or not. A store-bought frozen one works just as well.

INGREDIENTS

For the crust:
1 1/3 cups flour
1 tablespoon sugar
1/4 teaspoon salt
4 tablespoons (1/2 stick) unsalted butter
1/4 cup vegetable shortening (preferably one without trans fats)
2 tablespoons ice water

For the filling:
1 1/2 cups canned pumpkin puree, unsweetened
1/4 cup packed brown sugar
1/2 cup granulated sugar
1 1/2 cups evaporated milk
1/4 teaspoon salt
1 teaspoon ground cinnamon
1 teaspoon ground ginger
1 teaspoon ground nutmeg
1 teaspoon ground cloves
2 eggs

1. Preheat the oven to 425 degrees.

2. To make the crust, sift together the dry ingredients. Using a pastry blender or processor, cut in the butter and shortening until the mixture resembles coarse meal. Sprinkle the ice water over the dough and toss the mixture with a fork or your hands until the pastry is moist enough to form into a ball. Flatten the ball, wrap it in plastic wrap, and chill in the refrigerator for at least an hour.

3. Roll out the dough on a lightly floured surface into a 14-inch circle, then transfer this into a 9-inch pie pan, pressing it in. Trim the overhang and crimp the edges. Chill in the freezer for 15 minutes.

4. To make the pumpkin filling, whisk all the ingredients together in a large bowl until blended. Pour into the prepared crust.

5. Bake for 10 minutes, then reduce the oven to 350 degrees and bake for an additional 40 to 50 minutes, or until a knife inserted in the center comes out clean. Serve with whipped cream.

banana cream pie

SERVES 8 TO 10

Not all pies need to bake in the oven and cool on the windowsill. This recipe for banana cream pie—along with the following one, chocolate peanut butter pie—calls for an easy cookie crust and chilling instead of baking. You can mix and match the piecrusts with the fillings for variety.

INGREDIENTS

For the crust:
1 1/2 cups
   graham cracker crumbs
1/4 cup confectioners' sugar
1 teaspoon ground cinnamon
6 tablespoons unsalted
   butter, melted

For the filling:
2/3 cup sugar
1/3 cup all-purpose flour
1/4 teaspoon salt
2 cups milk
3 egg yolks, lightly beaten
2 tablespoons butter
2 teaspoons vanilla extract
2 ripe bananas

1. Make the crust: Mix the crushed graham crackers, sugar, cinnamon, and melted butter until well blended. Press the crumb mixture into a 10-inch pie plate. Freeze for 1 hour.

2. Prepare the filling: In a medium saucepan, combine the sugar, flour, and salt. Stir in the milk with a wooden spoon and cook over medium heat until the mixture starts to bubble and thicken. Be careful not to let it stick to the bottom of the pan. Remove from the heat.

3. Whisk in the egg yolks and stir until the mixture is smooth. Cook again over medium heat for about two minutes, until the mixture just comes to a boil, stirring constantly. Remove from the heat.

4. Stir in the butter and vanilla.

5. Cover the surface of the mixture with plastic wrap or waxed paper so that a skin doesn't form on top. Cool to room temperature.

banana cream pie

6. Assemble the pie: Slice the bananas and arrange them in the crust. Pour the filling on top, smooth with a spatula, then place in the refrigerator to chill for 4 to 6 hours.

7. Serve with whipped cream.

! **Variation:** Use crushed chocolate wafers instead of graham crackers for the crust.

Good apple pies
are a considerable
part of our domestic
happiness.

Jane Austen

chocolate peanut butter pie

SERVES 8 TO 10

INGREDIENTS

For the crust:
1 1/2 cups finely crushed
    vanilla wafers
2 tablespoons
    confectioners' sugar
6 tablespoons unsalted
    butter, melted

For the filling:
6 tablespoons cream cheese
6 tablespoons peanut butter
1/2 cup confectioners' sugar
3/4 cup nondairy
    whipped topping
1 package instant
    chocolate pudding mix
1 3/4 cups milk

For the garnish:
whipped cream
chocolate sprinkles

1. Mix the crushed cookies, sugar, and melted butter until well blended. Press the crumb mixture into a 10-inch pie plate. Freeze for 1 hour.

2. In a large bowl, beat cream cheese and peanut butter until fluffy. In two to three stages, gradually add the confectioners' sugar and whipped topping; continue to beat until smooth and creamy. Spoon into the piecrust and freeze for 30 to 60 minutes, until firm.

3. In a medium bowl, combine the instant pudding and milk. Beat with a fork until smooth. Spoon on top of the peanut butter layer and freeze for an additional 60 minutes, until firm.

4. Top with whipped cream and chocolate sprinkles.

lemon meringue pie

This is one of our favorite desserts in all the world. Of course you can make your own pastry—and we'll tell you how—but any supermarket will sell you one from its frozen-foods section. Do not stint on the grated lemon! This recipe is a little time consuming but incredibly good. The lemon filling can be made ahead and refrigerated. It will keep for more than a week.

INGREDIENTS
For the pastry tart shell:
1 cup all-purpose flour
1 tablespoon sugar
1/8 teaspoon salt
*1/2 teaspoon
    grated lemon zest*
*8 tablespoons (1 stick)
    unsalted butter, cut into
    bits*
*Approximately 1 1/2
    tablespoons cold water*

1. Prepare the pastry tart shell: In the bowl of an electric mixer or food processor, mix the flour, sugar, salt, and zest at low speed. Mix in the butter until the mixture is the consistency of cornmeal.

2. Add the water a little at a time, mixing until the pastry holds together. Wrap the pastry in plastic wrap and let it rest in the refrigerator for at least 30 minutes.

3. Preheat the oven to 375 degrees.

4. On a lightly floured countertop, roll out the dough into a 12-inch circle about 1/8 inch thick. (If the pastry sticks, use a little more flour on the counter and on the rolling pin.) Turn into a 9-inch pie pan. Lightly press the dough into the contours of the pan. Cut the pastry about 1/2 inch beyond the edge of the pan and crimp the edge with a fork. Prick the bottom of the pastry with the tines of a fork to keep it from puffing up in the oven. Refrigerate for

For the lemon filling:
1 whole large egg plus 3 large
egg yolks (save the whites
for the meringue)
1/3 cup sugar
Grated zest of 2 lemons
1/3 cup freshly squeezed lemon
juice (approximately 2
lemons), strained
2 tablespoons heavy cream
1/3 teaspoon cornstarch
5 1/3 tablespoons (1/3 cup)
unsalted butter, cut into bits

For the meringue:
3 egg whites (reserved from
the eggs used for the filling)
1/2 teaspoon lemon juice
1/2 teaspoon vanilla extract
3/4 cup plus 1 teaspoon sugar

30 minutes or until you're ready to bake. (Chilled dough shrinks less.)

5. Bake for 20 minutes or until light golden. Remove it from the oven and let it cool. The pie shell can be made ahead and frozen until you need it.

6. Prepare the filling: In a heavy, 2-quart saucepan, whisk together the egg, egg yolks, and sugar until well blended. Add the lemon zest and juice.

7. In a small bowl, blend together the heavy cream and cornstarch, then add to the egg mixture.

8. Place the saucepan over medium heat. Stirring constantly, add the butter, bit by bit. Cook until the mixture thickens and just comes to a boil. Be very careful not to let it burn. Take it off the heat as soon as you see your first bubble!

9. Pour the filling into the baked and cooled tart shell, or refrigerate for future use.

10. Prepare the meringue: In the bowl of an electric mixer, beat the egg whites until frothy, then beat in the lemon juice and vanilla and slowly increase the speed. Gradually add 3/4 cup of the sugar and beat until glossy, stiff peaks form.

11. Mound the meringue over the filling and swirl it into peaks. Spread the meringue so that it touches the edges of the crust.

12. Sprinkle with remaining teaspoon of sugar and bake in a 375-degree oven for about 15 minutes or until the meringue is lightly browned. Let the pie cool to room temperature before refrigerating.

peach and berry cobbler

SERVES 6 TO 8

This can be made in the morning, cooled, covered with plastic, and refrigerated before warming and serving. You can use almost any fruit or combination of fruits: apples, pears, plums, blueberries, strawberries—whatever is in season— and it always works. Double the recipe for big parties.

INGREDIENTS

7 peaches, peeled and sliced
2 pints (4 cups) raspberries
1/3 cup sugar,
    plus extra for sprinkling
2 tablespoons
    fresh lemon juice
Zest of 1 lemon, finely grated
2 cups all-purpose flour
2 teaspoons baking powder
3/4 teaspoon salt
10 tablespoons (1 1/4 sticks)
    cold unsalted butter,
    cut into 1/2-inch cubes
3/4 cup whole milk

1. Preheat the oven to 375 degrees.

2. Butter a 12- by 10-inch glass baking dish.

3. In a large bowl, combine the fruit, sugar, lemon juice, and zest. Mix well and pour into the greased baking dish.

4. In another bowl, mix together the flour, baking powder, and salt. Use a pastry blender or two knives to work in the butter. The mixture should have the texture of coarse bread crumbs.

5. Stir in the milk. Drop the mixture on top of the fruit by heaping tablespoons.

6. Sprinkle lightly with sugar and bake about 40 minutes, until nicely browned.

7. Serve immediately, topped with vanilla ice cream!

strawberry shortcake

SERVES 8 TO 10

This is a great dessert for entertaining because you can bake the cake ahead of time, and then assemble at the last minute. It is one of our favorite desserts to serve in the summer, when local strawberries are available.

INGREDIENTS

For the shortcake:
3 cups sugar
1 cup (2 sticks) unsalted
    butter, room temperature
6 eggs
1 cup (8 ounces) sour cream
2 tablespoons vanilla extract
4 cups flour
1/4 teaspoon salt
1/2 teaspoon baking soda

For the whipped cream:
3 cups heavy cream
1/2 cup granulated sugar

For the fruit:
2 pints (4 cups)
    fresh strawberries

1. Make the shortcake: Preheat the oven to 350 degrees. Butter and flour two round cake pans, 8 or 9 inches in diameter. Set aside.

2. In a large bowl, cream together the sugar and butter. Beat in the eggs one at a time, scraping the bowl with a rubber spatula between additions. Add the sour cream and vanilla, mixing well.

3. In a separate bowl, combine the flour, salt, and baking soda. Add to the egg mixture and blend.

4. Pour into the prepared pans. Bake for 1 to 1 1/4 hours, or until the cakes are browned and the surface bounces back when touched lightly with a fingertip. Let the cakes cool for 30 minutes before turning them out of the pans. Set them aside and let them cool completely.

strawberry shortcake

5. While the cakes are cooling, prepare the whipped cream. Put the cream and sugar into a large bowl (chill it first if your kitchen is very warm). Using a hand mixer or whisk, whip the cream with the sugar until soft peaks form. (Do not overwhip, or the cream will start to coagulate and develop a waxy feel on the tongue.) Refrigerate until you are ready to assemble the cake.

6. Prepare the fruit: Rinse, trim, and halve the strawberries. Set them aside to dry on paper towels.

7. Once the cakes are cool, you can begin assembly. Slice each cake in half horizontally so that your shortcake has a total of four layers. Spread whipped cream over one layer, top with strawberries and the next layer of cake, and repeat to build your cake.

✳ **Note:** The shortcakes may be prepared up to 24 hours ahead of time, and the strawberries and whipped cream can be prepared several hours ahead. But the dessert itself should not be assembled until less than an hour before serving, to prevent sogginess.

❗ **Variation–Peach Shortcake:** Fresh, juicy peaches, in season, combined with a squeeze of lemon juice and sugar, are also delicious in this cake.

apple crisp

SERVES 8 TO 10

We had a version of this (with the cranberries) at Mustards, a great restaurant in Napa Valley. Nectarines or plums can be substituted for apples, with delicious results. Now we make it every year for Thanksgiving as well as for a potluck or two.

INGREDIENTS

For the filling:
9 Granny Smith apples,
 peeled, cored,
 and cut into slices
Juice of 2 lemons
1/2 cup sugar

For the topping:
1 cup rolled oats
1 1/2 cups packed
 brown sugar
1/2 cup all-purpose flour
1 teaspoon ground cinnamon
1/2 teaspoon ground nutmeg
8 tablespoons (1 stick)
 unsalted butter,
 cut into pieces
1/2 cup walnuts,
 in large pieces

1. Preheat the oven to 375 degrees.

2. Mix together the apples, lemon juice, and sugar. Spread the filling mixture evenly into a 9- by 13- by 2-inch baking dish.

3. Mix together the oats, brown sugar, flour, cinnamon, and nutmeg. Add the butter and toss it with the flour mixture. Using your fingers, rub the flour mixture and the butter together to form large "crumbs." Add the nuts and toss again.

4. Sprinkle the topping mixture over the apples. Bake for about 45 minutes, until the apples are cooked through and the top has browned. Let cool for 15 minutes. Serve with vanilla ice cream.

! **Variation—Apple-Cranberry Crisp:** Substitute 2 cups fresh or frozen whole cranberries for two of the apples for a delicious twist on this classic.

apple cake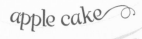

SERVES 8

This easy-to-make cake—which is really an upside-down cake—goes perfectly with an afternoon cup of coffee, or with ice cream, if you want to serve it as a real dessert. The recipe is adapted from one that we found in *Cook's Country* magazine.

INGREDIENTS

For the apple topping:
3 tablespoons unsalted butter
1/2 cup packed
    light brown sugar
3 large Granny Smith
    apples, peeled,
    cored, and cut into
    1/4-inch slices
1/8 teaspoon salt

For the cake:
1/2 cup sour cream, divided
1 large egg plus 1 egg yolk
1/2 teaspoon vanilla extract
1 1/4 cups all-purpose flour
3/4 cup sugar
1/2 teaspoon baking powder
1/4 teaspoon baking soda
1/4 teaspoon ground cinnamon
1/4 teaspoon salt
8 tablespoons (1 stick)
    butter, cut into pieces

1. Preheat the oven to 350 degrees. Lightly grease a 9-inch cake pan.

2. Make the apple topping: Melt the butter in a large, heavy skillet over medium heat. Add the light brown sugar and cook until the sugar turns brown.

3. Stir the apples and salt into the sugar-butter mixture. Cook for 5 to 7 minutes, or until the apples have softened slightly. Pour this mixture into the prepared pan.

4. Prepare the cake: In a small bowl, whisk together 1/4 cup of the sour cream with the egg, yolk, and vanilla.

5. In a large mixing bowl, sift together the flour, sugar, baking powder, baking soda, cinnamon, and salt.

6. Add the butter and the remaining 1/4 cup sour cream and mix well to moisten. Add the egg–sour cream mixture and beat until the batter is fluffy.

apple cake

7. Spread the batter gently over the apples. Bake until the cake is golden brown and a toothpick comes out clean when inserted into the center, about 35 to 40 minutes.

8. Place a serving platter over the top of the pan and invert. The cake will detach itself. This is best served warm.

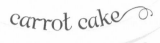

carrot cake

SERVES 8 TO 10

INGREDIENTS

1 ½ cups vegetable oil
2 cups sugar
3 cups flour
4 eggs
2 teaspoons
   ground cinnammon
2 teaspoons baking powder
2 teaspoons baking soda
3 cups grated carrots
1 cup unsweetened applesauce
1 teaspoon salt
1 cup raisins (optional)
1 cup walnuts, chopped
   (optional)

1. Preheat the oven to 350 degrees. Grease and flour two 9-inch round cake pans and set them aside.

2. In separate bowls, mix together the dry ingredients and wet ingredients. Combine and mix well. Add the raisins and walnuts, if using.

3. Pour into the baking pans and bake for 25 to 30 minutes, or until a toothpick or fork comes out clean.

4. Let the cakes cool in the pans for 5 minutes, and then turn them out onto cooling racks.

5. When the layers are completely cool, frost them with Cream Cheese Icing (below). The cake can be served immediately or refrigerated overnight.

cream cheese frosting

8 ounces cream cheese,
   softened
8 tablespoons (1 stick)
   unsalted butter, softened
1 teaspoon vanilla extract
1 (16-ounce) box
   confectioners' sugar

With an electric mixer, blend together the cream cheese, butter, vanilla, and sugar until fluffy.

classic layer cake

MAKES ONE 8- OR 9-INCH CAKE

This dense vanilla cake, layered with rich chocolate icing, is the perfect birthday cake.

vanilla cake

INGREDIENTS
2 1/2 cups cake or
   all-purpose flour, sifted
1 1/2 cups sugar
1 tablespoon baking powder
1 teaspoon salt
8 tablespoons (1 stick)
   unsalted butter, room
   temperature
1 cup milk, divided
1 tablespoon vanilla extract
2 eggs

1. Preheat the oven to 350 degrees. Butter and flour two round cake pans, 8 or 9 inches in diameter.

2. In a large bowl, mix together the flour, sugar, baking powder, and salt.

3. Continue to mix, slowly adding the butter, 2/3 cup of the milk, and the vanilla. Beat vigorously.

4. Add the remaining 1/3 cup milk along with the eggs. Beat for 2 minutes, then pour into the baking pans. Bake for 30 to 35 minutes. Let the cakes cool before turning them out of the pans.

5. When the cakes are completely cool, frost.

chocolate icing

INGREDIENTS
8 tablespoons (1 stick)
   unsalted butter
4 squares unsweetened
   baking chocolate
1 (2-pound) box
   confectioners' sugar
1 tablespoon vanilla extract
1/3 cup milk

1. Melt the butter and chocolate together in a small saucepan.

2. Pour the mixture into a large bowl, add the remaining ingredients, and beat until smooth.

devil's food cupcakes
with vanilla frosting

MAKES 24 CUPCAKES

This is an excellent recipe for a chocolate "from-scratch" cake. The key to making a tender cake is real cake flour—available in the baking section of most grocery stores—and you must avoid overmixing the batter. This recipe was adapted from Faye Levy's award-winning cookbook *Chocolate Sensations*.

INGREDIENTS

2 cups cake flour
2/3 cup cocoa powder (unsweetened)
1 1/4 teaspoons baking soda
1/4 teaspoon salt
1/2 cup buttermilk
1/3 cup water
12 tablespoons (1 1/2 sticks) unsalted butter, softened
1 3/4 cups sugar
2 large eggs
1 1/2 teaspoons vanilla extract

1. Preheat the oven to 350 degrees. Line 24 muffin cups with paper liners (or line one 12-cup muffin tin and repeat after the first batch is done).

2. Sift together the flour, cocoa, baking soda, and salt into a large bowl. Mix the buttermilk and water in a small bowl.

3. Using an electric mixer, cream the butter in a large bowl. Add the sugar and beat until smooth. Add the eggs, one at a time, and the vanilla. Scrape the bowl between additions. Beat until well blended.

4. Slowly blend in about a quarter of the cocoa mixture, then about a third of the buttermilk mixture. Repeat three times until cocoa and buttermilk are used up. Do not overmix.

devil's food cupcakes
with vanilla frosting

5. Fill the baking cups about two-thirds full—you'll use about $^1/4$ cup of batter for each. Bake for approximately 20 minutes, until the tops of the cupcakes spring back when touched lightly with your finger.

6. When the cupcakes are cool, top each with Vanilla Frosting.

vanilla frosting

INGREDIENTS
1 pound confectioners' sugar
12 tablespoons (1 $^1/2$ sticks) unsalted butter, softened
1 $^1/2$ teaspoons vanilla extract
3 tablespoons milk

Using an electric mixer, beat together all the ingredients until smooth. If the mixture is too stiff to spread easily, add a little more milk.

flourless chocolate cake

SERVES 10

There are lots of reasons why flourless chocolate cake shows up on so many restaurant menus: It's so easy, keeps well, and can be dressed up with almost any flavor of ice cream—or just a puff of confectioners' sugar. Don't be alarmed when the center of the cake collapses as it cools. It's the perfect place to put a soft mound of whipped cream and some berries or shaved chocolate.

INGREDIENTS
8 ounces high-quality
  bittersweet chocolate,
  chopped
8 tablespoons (1 stick)
  unsalted butter
6 large eggs
1 cup sugar, divided
2 teaspoons vanilla extract

1. Preheat the oven to 350 degrees. Line the bottom of an 8-inch springform pan with a round of waxed paper or baking parchment. Do not butter the pan.

2. Melt the chocolate in a bowl set over simmering water. Whisk in the butter and remove from the heat.

3. Separate 4 of the eggs into two mixing bowls. (Make sure that the bowl into which you put the egg whites is scrupulously clean and grease free, or else the whites won't come out light and airy.)

4. To the bowl of yolks, add the two remaining eggs and $1/2$ cup of the sugar. Whisk to blend, then add the melted chocolate mixture and vanilla. Beat until blended.

flourless chocolate cake

5. Using an electric mixer, beat the egg whites until they become foamy. When they reach this stage, slowly add the remaining 1/2 cup sugar. (If you add the sugar too fast, the whites will be runny. If you add it too slowly, they will become too dry and airy and will be difficult to mix into the chocolate.) Beat until they form soft, moist peaks.

6. Stir about a third of the whites into the chocolate mixture to make it lighter, then gently fold in the rest.

7. Pour the batter into the pan, and bake for 35 to 40 minutes, until the top is puffed and cracked. (It's better to underbake this cake than overbake it, so: "If in doubt, take it out!")

8. Serve warm-ish or at room temperature.

cheese blintzes

MAKES ABOUT 25 BLINTZES

One of our best family friends makes these "blintzes" every year for her Oscar party. Nevertheless it took us years to get the recipe from her! We always quadruple the recipe, because they freeze and keep well for a long time—although we rarely have any left over.

INGREDIENTS

8 slices Wonder™ White Bread (has to be Wonder)
1 (8-ounce) package cream cheese (or use whipped cream cheese)
1 teaspoon vanilla extract
1 egg yolk
2 tablespoons sugar, plus 1 cup for coating
1 teaspoon ground cinnamon
8 tablespoons (1 stick) unsalted butter, melted
1 pint (2 cups) sour cream, for serving

1. Preheat the oven to 350 degrees. (If you're going to freeze the blintzes for the future, skip this step.)

2. Cut the crusts from the bread. Using a rolling pin, flatten the pieces of bread as thin as possible.

3. Blend together the cream cheese, vanilla, egg yolk, and 2 tablespoons sugar.

4. Spread the cream-cheese mixture onto a flattened slice of bread, then roll the bread into a log.

5. Combine the remaining cup of sugar with the cinnamon. Dip the log into the melted butter, then roll it in the cinnamon sugar. (At this point you can freeze the logs, wrapped tightly in foil; when you're ready to serve, let them thaw for about 10 minutes.)

6. Cut each log into three pieces and place these on an ungreased cookie sheet.

7. Bake for about 10 to 15 minutes or until brown. Serve with a bowl of sour cream and stand clear of the stampede.

new york cheesecake

SERVES 8 TO 12

INGREDIENTS

For the crust:
20 cinnamon
    graham crackers
5 tablespoons sugar
6 tablespoons unsalted butter,
    melted

For the cheese filling:
4 (8-ounce) packages cream
    cheese, room temperature,
    divided
1²/3 cups sugar, divided
¹/4 cup cornstarch
2 extra-large eggs
³/4 cup heavy cream
1 tablespoon vanilla extract

For the topping:
12 ounces sour cream
2 tablespoons sugar

1. Prepare the crust: Preheat the oven to 350 degrees. Wrap the outside of a 10-inch springform pan in a double sheet of foil (the cake will be baked in a water bath, and this will prevent water from seeping in).

2. Place the crackers in a blender or food processor and grind them into crumbs. (Or you can place them in a sealed plastic bag and crush with a rolling pin.)

3. In a bowl, combine the crumbs, sugar, and melted butter. Press the mixture along the bottom and sides of the springform pan.

4. Bake for 8 to 10 minutes. Remove from the oven and set aside.

5. Prepare the filling: Place one package of cream cheese, ¹/3 cup sugar, and the cornstarch in a large bowl; beat on low speed with an electric mixer until smooth. Increase the speed to high. Add the remaining cream cheese and sugar and beat until the mixture is smooth and light.

new york cheesecake

6. Add the eggs one at a time. Scrape down the sides of the mixing bowl with a rubber spatula. Add the heavy cream and vanilla. Beat only until combined. Do not overmix.

7. Pour the mixture into the prepared crust.

8. Place the springform pan in a large shallow pan containing hot water that comes to about 1 inch up the sides of the pan. Tent with aluminum foil.

9. Bake the cheescake until the center barely jiggles when you shake the pan, about an hour. Remove the springform pan from the hot-water bath and cool to room temperature, then place it in the refrigerator until it's thoroughly chilled, at least 4 hours.

10. Make the topping by combining the sour cream and sugar. Spread this evenly over the cheesecake and refrigerate for at least an hour longer. Slice and serve.

honeycake

SERVES 10 TO 12

Make this cake a day ahead if you can; the flavors of the spices will become more apparent.

INGREDIENTS

1 tablespoon unsalted butter, softened, for greasing pan
3 large eggs
1 cup sugar
1 cup honey
1/2 cup brewed espresso, cooled
1 cup vegetable oil
1 teaspoon vanilla extract
2 1/2 cups sifted all-purpose flour
2 teaspoons baking powder
1/2 teaspoon baking soda
1/4 teaspoon salt
1 teaspoon ground cinnamon
1/2 teaspoon ground cloves
1/2 teaspoon ground allspice
1/4 teaspoon ground ginger
1/2 cup chopped hazelnuts or walnuts
Zest of 1/4 orange
1 tablespoon cognac
1 to 2 tablespoons confectioners' sugar, for dusting

1. Preheat the oven to 350 degrees. Butter a bundt pan or 9-inch square baking pan.

2. Whisk together the eggs, sugar, honey, espresso, vegetable oil, and vanilla.

3. Sift together the flour, baking powder, baking soda, salt, cinnamon, cloves, allspice, and ginger.

4. Combine the egg mixture with the dry ingredients and mix well.

5. Stir in the nuts, orange zest, and cognac.

6. Pour the batter into the prepared pan and bake in the center of the oven for 45 to 55 minutes, or until the cake springs back when lightly touched and a toothpick comes out clean. Cool on a wire rack.

7. Dust with confectioners' sugar and serve.

vermont whiskey cake

SERVES 8 TO 10

Baking doesn't get much easier or better than this. This cake is so simple and delicious, you'll probably make it again and again throughout the year! You can use a bundt-cake mold or loaf pan, or make individual cakes using mini bundt molds or cupcake pans.

INGREDIENTS
For the cake:
1 box yellow cake mix
1 box instant vanilla pudding
1 cup water
1/2 cup salad oil
4 eggs

For the whiskey mixture:
1/2 cup sugar
4 tablespoons (1/2 stick)
* unsalted butter*
1/2 cup whiskey

1. Preheat the oven to 350 degrees. Thoroughly grease and flour your cake pan(s).

2. Prepare the cake by mixing all the ingredients together until smooth.

3. Pour into the pan(s) and bake for an hour, or until the top springs back after being touched lightly with a fingertip and a toothpick, stuck into the cake, comes out clean.

4. Meanwhile, prepare the whiskey mixture by melting together the sugar, butter, and whiskey in a small pan over low heat.

5. Remove the cake from the oven. Spoon the whiskey mixture over the cake slowly, letting it sink in.

6. Return the cake to the oven and bake for another 5 minutes.

7. Cool and remove from the pan(s).

ice cream

Let's face it, there's nothing more comforting than ice cream, even if you eat it with a spoon straight out of the container. But if you are willing to make just a little bit of an effort, here are some great alternatives.

banana split
SERVES 2 OR 3

INGREDIENTS
1 banana
3 scoops favorite ice cream
flavors (traditionally
chocolate, vanilla, and
strawberry)
1/2 cup chocolate fudge sauce
1 cup whipped cream
(see page 256)
2 tablespoons
chopped walnuts
1 maraschino cherry

1. Peel the banana and slice it lengthwise. Place the banana halves flat-side up in the bottom of a sundae dish.

2. Add the ice cream scoops side by side on top of the banana. Cover in chocolate sauce.

3. Garnish with whipped cream, nuts, and finally the cherry on top!

ice cream

hot fudge sundae

SERVES 1

2 scoops ice cream
¹/₂ cup chocolate fudge sauce
¹/₂ cup whipped cream
1 tablespoon chopped walnuts
1 maraschino cherry

1. In a small pot, heat the chocolate fudge sauce on medium-high heat until it begins to bubble. Remove from heat.

2. Place the ice-cream scoops in a deep bowl.

3. Layer the hot fudge sauce, whipped cream, nuts, and cherry on top. Serve immediately!

ice cream sandwiches

MAKES 12 SANDWICHES

1 gallon vanilla or chocolate ice cream, slightly softened
2 dozen chocolate chip cookies (see the recipe on page 112)
2 cups mini chocolate chips or sprinkles

1. Place and carefully flatten a scoop of ice cream on a cookie. Top with a second cookie and press down. Roll the sides in chips or sprinkles. Place in a freezer bag and freeze immediately.

2. Allow the sandwiches to freeze for at least two hours before serving. These will keep for up to a week in the freezer.

strawberry ice cream pie

SERVES 8 TO 10

INGREDIENTS

For the crust:
1 1/2 cups finely crushed Oreo cookie crumbs
3 tablespoons unsalted butter, melted

For the filling:
2 cups strawberry ice cream, softened
2 cups vanilla ice cream, softened
16 large marshmallows
16 ounces frozen strawberries, thawed, with juice
1 cup heavy cream
1/4 cup sugar

1. Mix the cookie crumbs and butter until well blended. Press the crumbs firmly into a 10-inch pie plate and place in the freezer for 30 minutes.

2. Fill the bottom of the piecrust with strawberry ice cream. Freeze until firm (about 30 minutes).

3. Add a layer of vanilla ice cream on top of the strawberry layer. Freeze again until firm (about 30 minutes).

4. In a saucepan, combine the marshmallows with 2 to 3 tablespoons of juice from the strawberries. Stir over medium heat until melted. (Alternatively, you can coat the marshmallows with juice from the strawberries in a microwavable bowl and microwave on high for about 1 1/2 minutes, or until melted.) Cool.

5. Fold the strawberries into the cooled marshmallows. Spread the mixture onto the pie over the vanilla ice cream layer. Freeze again until firm.

6. When you're ready to serve, whip the cream and sugar together until stiff. Spoon onto the pie and serve immediately.

mocha-toffee ice cream pie

SERVES 8 TO 10

INGREDIENTS

For the crust:
1 1/2 cups finely crushed
  cookie crumbs, made from
  your favorite sandwich
  cookies
3 tablespoons unsalted butter,
  melted

For the filling:
2 cups coffee ice cream,
  softened
12 ounces caramel topping,
  store-bought (dulce de
  leche is excellent)
2 cups chocolate ice cream,
  softened
2 cups nondairy whipped
  topping, thawed
1 English toffee bar, crumbled

1. Mix the cookie crumbs and butter until well blended. Press the crumbs firmly into a 9-inch pie plate.

2. Spoon the coffee ice cream into the crust and spread evenly. Freeze until firm, about 15 minutes.

3. Spread half of the caramel topping on top of the coffee ice cream.

4. Spread the chocolate ice cream on top of the caramel layer. Freeze until firm, about 15 minutes.

5. Spread the remaining caramel topping on top of the pie. Arrange dollops of whipped topping in a circular pattern on top of the caramel layer and sprinkle with the crumbled toffee bar. Freeze the pie until firm, at least five hours.

6. Let the pie stand at room temperature for at least 15 minutes before serving.

Tiramisu

SERVES 8

This is the Italian dessert that no two restaurants make the same—but that everyone loves no matter how it's made. This is the simplest version to make at home. It makes a heavenly dessert for a Valentine dinner with your friends.

INGREDIENTS
2 cups (16 ounces) mascarpone (Italian cream cheese), room temperature
1/2 cup confectioners' sugar
1 cup (1/2 pint) heavy cream, chilled
1 teaspoon vanilla extract
1 1/2 cups brewed espresso coffee, cooled, or 1 table-spoon instant espresso dissolved in 1 1/2 cups boiling water and then cooled
1 1/2 cups sweet Marsala (you can substitute dark rum)
1 (7-ounce) package Italian dry ladyfingers (biscotti di savoiardi)
1 to 2 ounces dark bitter-sweet chocolate or unsweetened cocoa powder, for garnish

1. Blend the mascarpone and sugar together until smooth.

2. Whip the cream with the vanilla until soft peaks form.

3. Fold the whipped cream and mascarpone together.

4. Mix the espresso and liquor together in a shallow dish.

5. Take half of the ladyfingers and dip them briefly (on both sides) in the espresso mixture.

6. Arrange them in a single layer in a 7- by 11-inch serving dish and spread with half the mascarpone mixture.

7. Add a second layer of espresso-dipped ladyfingers and spread with the remaining mascarpone.

8. Cover tightly with plastic wrap and chill for at least four hours. Overnight is fine, too.

9. When you're ready to serve, grate the chocolate (or dust the cocoa powder) over the top.

chocolate mousse

SERVES 6 TO 8

Make this the night before in a glass bowl or individual champagne flutes. Serve with berries and/or whipped cream.

INGREDIENTS

6 ounces (three 2-ounce squares) really good semi-sweet chocolate, finely chopped

4 eggs

3 teaspoons sugar, divided

¼ cup strong espresso

2 tablespoons dark rum (optional)

1 cup (approximately ½ pint) very cold heavy cream

1. At least one hour ahead of time, place a stainless-steel mixing bowl in the freezer.

2. Melt the chocolate in a double boiler.

3. Separate the eggs. Combine the yolks and 2 teaspoons of the sugar in a bowl and beat until pale yellow and creamy. Add the melted chocolate, coffee, and rum; mix together with a rubber spatula or wooden spoon until uniformly combined.

4. Take the mixing bowl from the freezer and add the cream. Beat until it is thickened and forms soft mounds, then fold it into the chocolate-egg mixture.

5. In a scrupulously clean bowl, whip the egg whites with the remaining teaspoon of sugar until they form soft peaks; fold them gently but thoroughly into chocolate mousse mixture.

6. Spoon the mousse into individual serving cups or one large bowl, cover with plastic wrap, and refrigerate overnight.

7. Serve with whipped cream or raspberries, or both.

classic rice pudding

SERVES 6

This is comfort food at its finest. As a kid I think I went for weeks once eating nothing but rice pudding (but I picked out the raisins). This is our grandmother's recipe. KF

INGREDIENTS
2 quarts whole milk
3/4 cup long-grain rice
3 eggs
1/2 cup white sugar
1 cup whole milk
1 teaspoon vanilla extract
3/4 cup raisins
1 tablespoon
  ground cinnamon

1. Pour 2 quarts milk into a large saucepan and bring to a boil over medium heat. Reduce heat to low, then mix in rice and simmer uncovered for 20 minutes, stirring frequently and skimming surface of milk as needed.

2. In a medium bowl, whisk together eggs, sugar, milk, and vanilla extract. Slowly pour into rice mixture while stirring vigorously. Allow mixture to boil and thicken, approximately 10 minutes, while stirring constantly.

3. Remove from heat and stir in raisins. Pour mixture into a 9- by 13-inch pan and sprinkle cinnamon over top. Allow to cool uncovered in refrigerator for a few hours, until pudding is chilled and firm. Cover with plastic wrap when cool.

bread pudding

SERVES 8

What's not to like about bread, eggs, sugar, and cream, except, perhaps, the calories? If you really want to gild the lily, serve it with warmed, store-bought caramel sauce or dulce de leche. (We, however, are perfectly content with a bit of cold heavy cream poured over the top!) Make sure the cubes of bread are on the large side—about 3/4-inch square.

INGREDIENTS
3 1/2 cups cubed stale bread (preferably challah or brioche, but other plain breads will work as well)
1/2 cup dried currants (optional)
4 large eggs
2 large egg yolks
2/3 cup sugar
1/8 teaspoon salt
3 cups half-and-half (or whole milk)
2 teaspoons vanilla extract or 1/2 vanilla bean, split in half vertically, seeds scraped out
1/2 teaspoon ground cinnamon
Fresh nutmeg to taste

1. Preheat the oven to 375 degrees. Butter a 2-quart baking dish (such as a soufflé dish). Toss together the bread cubes and currants (if using) in the baking dish and set aside.

2. In a large mixing bowl, whisk together the eggs, egg yolks, sugar, and salt.

3. Put a teakettle of water on the stove to boil.

4. In a heavy saucepan, heat the half-and-half with the vanilla extract or vanilla bean until tiny bubbles start to form around the edges of the pan and the mixture is very hot. (Remove the vanilla bean, rinse it, and store it wrapped in plastic or buried in sugar, for future use.)

5. Ladle about a cup of hot half-and-half into the egg mixture, whisking constantly, to temper the eggs. Add the rest of the half-and-half to the eggs, whisking to blend.

bread pudding

6. Strain the egg mixture through a sieve over the bread in the baking dish. Sprinkle the top with the cinnamon and nutmeg. Cover with foil. Place the dish inside a 13- by 9- by 2-inch (or similarly sized) baking pan and place in the oven. Pour boiling water into the larger pan, to the height of about 1 inch up the side of the baking dish, and close the oven door.

7. Remove the foil from the top of the pudding after 50 minutes. Check to see if the pudding is set. It should just tremble a bit in the middle when it's done. Leave it in the oven a bit longer if it seems too wobbly. This pudding is delicious served hot or cold.

* **Note:** If you want a more elegant presentation, bake the pudding in a square or rectangular pan so that you can easily cut it into squares or rectangles.

Food is not about
impressing people.
It's about making
them feel comfortable.

Ina Garten

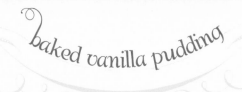

baked vanilla pudding

SERVES 6

This dessert is so high on the list of comforting dishes that it's sometimes referred to as "nursery food."

INGREDIENTS
3 eggs, slightly beaten
1 egg yolk
¼ cup sugar
¼ teaspoon salt
1 teaspoon vanilla extract
2 cups half-and-half, whole milk, or skim milk, scalded
Freshly ground nutmeg, for garnish

1. Put a teakettle of water on the stove to boil and preheat the oven to 325 degrees.

2. In a medium bowl, whisk together the eggs, egg yolk, sugar, salt, and vanilla.

3. Gradually add the half-and-half or milk. Pour into six (6-ounce) custard cups. Sprinkle with freshly grated nutmeg.

4. Place the custard cups in a large baking pan; pour boiling water into the pan to a depth of 1 inch. Bake for 40 to 45 minutes or until a knife inserted halfway between the center and the edge of a cup comes out clean. Remove the cups from the water and cool. May be eaten warm or chilled.

chocolate pudding

SERVES 4

This creamy treat is infinitely better than instant and ridiculously easy to make. My dad, George, didn't cook, but having been brought up in a highly cultured Hungarian family, he adored sweets and had great culinary taste. When I was eight years old, he found a little Hungarian restaurant a few blocks from home where we went often for chocolate pudding. LT

INGREDIENTS
*3/4 cup chocolate chips,
   the best you can find*
1/2 cup granulated sugar
2 cups whole milk
3 tablespoons cornstarch
Pinch of salt
1/2 tablespoon vanilla extract
1 cup heavy cream
*1 teaspoon vanilla sugar
   (or sugar)*

1. In a heavy saucepan, combine the chocolate, sugar, and milk. Heat slowly over a medium flame, whisking constantly until the chocolate is melted and smooth. Be careful not to let the mixture boil.

2. Turn off the heat and pour half of the heated mixture into a bowl. Add the cornstarch and salt and whisk until combined. Pour back into the saucepan.

3. Keep stirring as you continue cooking over low heat until the mixture thickens, about 8 to 10 minutes.

4. Remove it from the heat, add the vanilla, and let it cool. You can accelerate the cooling by putting the saucepan in the refrigerator.

5. In a bowl, mix the heavy cream and vanilla sugar. Whip with a whisk or electric mixer until stiff.

6. Once the pudding has cooled, serve it in a large bowl or in smaller individual bowls, and top with whipped cream.

pineapple upside-down cake

SERVES 8

INGREDIENTS

For the topping:
1 (16-ounce) can pineapple
   slices, juice reserved
1 1/2 cups
   packed brown sugar
8 tablespoons (1 stick)
   unsalted butter, melted

For the cake:
2 1/4 cups cake flour, sifted
1 1/2 cups sugar
1 teaspoon salt
1 tablespoon baking powder
8 tablespoons (1 stick) butter,
   softened
3/4 cup juice
   from the pineapple can
1/4 cup milk
2 medium eggs

1. Preheat the oven to 350 degrees.

2. Generously butter a 13- by 9- by 2-inch baking pan, then line it with parchment paper. Coat the paper with butter.

3. Prepare the topping by placing pineapple slices in a pleasing arrangement in the prepared pan. Cover the slices with the brown sugar, then pour the melted butter atop.

4. Make the cake: In a large mixing bowl, sift together the flour, sugar, salt, and baking powder.

5. Add the butter and pineapple juice; beat on medium speed for 2 minutes, scraping the bowl often. Add the milk and eggs; beat for 2 more minutes.

6. Pour the batter into the pan, spreading it evenly over the pineapple.

pineapple upside-down cake

Bake for 40 minutes or until the cake springs back
when lightly touched in the center. Let it sit for 2
to 3 minutes.

7. Run a knife around the inside edges of the pan to
loosen. Place a serving platter on top of the cake
and invert. Carefully remove the parchment while
the cake is still hot. Cool before serving.

kugel

SERVES 8 TO 10

INGREDIENTS

1 pound uncooked egg noodles
8 tablespoons (1 stick)
  unsalted butter,
  cut into pieces
1 cup sugar
4 large eggs
1/2 pound cottage cheese,
  pot style
1 pint (2 cups) sour cream
2 cups milk
1 (24-ounce) can peaches,
  cut into bite-size pieces
  (drain syrup)
1 teaspoon vanilla extract
1/2 (12-ounce) jar
  orange marmalade
1/2 cup golden raisins
1/2 cup cornflakes
2 tablespoons cinnamon
  sugar (1/2 tablespoon
  cinnamon plus 1 1/2
  tablespoons sugar)

1. Preheat the oven to 350 degrees.

2. Parboil the noodles (5 minutes) in 4 quarts of salted water and drain.

3. Toss the hot noodles with the butter, making sure that the butter completely melts and the noodles are thoroughly coated.

4. In a large bowl, whisk together the sugar and eggs, either by hand or with a hand mixer. Add the cheese, sour cream, and milk.

5. Fold in the peaches, vanilla, marmalade, and raisins. Add the noodles and mix thoroughly.

6. Pour everything into an 11- by 7- by 2-inch baking dish. Fill the dish three-quarters of the way to the rim, allowing space for the pudding to rise.

7. Lightly sprinkle crushed cornflakes over the top of the pudding. Sprinkle with cinnamon sugar.

8. Bake for 1 hour. Noodle pudding can be frozen and reheated.

LIQUID MEASURES

¹/₄ cup = 2 fluid ounces = ¹/₈ pint = 59 ml = 4 tablespoons

¹/₂ cup = 4 fluid ounces = ¹/₄ pint = 118 ml = 8 tablespoons

1 cup = 8 fluid ounces = ¹/₂ pint = 237 ml = 16 tablespoons

2 cups = 16 fluid ounces = 1 pint = 473 ml

4 cups = 32 fluid ounces = 1 quart = 946 ml

2 pints = 32 fluid ounces = 1 quart = 946 ml

4 quarts = 128 fluid ounces = 1 gallon = 3.785 liters

DRY MEASURES

3 teaspoons = 1 tablespoon = ¹/₂ ounce = 14.3 grams

2 tablespoons = ¹/₈ cup = 1 fluid ounce = 28.35 grams

4 tablespoons = ¹/₄ cup = 2 fluid ounces = 56.7 grams

5 ¹/₃ tablespoons = ¹/₃ cup = 2.6 fluid ounces = 75.6 grams

8 tablespoons = ¹/₂ cup = 4 ounces = 113.4 grams

12 tablespoons = ³/₄ cup = 6 ounces = .375 pounds = 170 grams

32 tablespoons = 2 cups = 16 ounces = 1 pound = 453.6 grams

64 tablespoons = 4 cups = 32 ounces = 2 pounds = 907 grams

COMMON SUBSTITUTIONS

Baking Powder, 1 teaspoon= ¹/₄ teaspoon baking soda plus 1/2 teaspoon cream of tartar

Baking Soda=There is no substitute!

Broth (beef or chicken), 1 cup = 1 cup hot water and 1 teaspoon instant bouillon (or 1 bouillon cube)

Brown sugar, 1 cup = 1 cup sugar, 2 tablespoons molasses

Butter, 1 cup = 1 cup regular margarine or 1 cup trans-fat free vegetable shortening (for baking) = same amount of olive oil can also be substituted in cooking (but not baking)

Buttermilk, 1 cup = 1 cup plain yogurt = 1 tablespoon lemon juice or vinegar plus enough whole milk to make one cup

Chocolate, unsweetened, 1 ounce = 3 tablespoons cocoa plus 1 tablespoon butter or margarine or vegetable oil

Cornstarch (when used for thickening), 1 tablespoon = 2 tablespoons flour

Cream, heavy, 1 cup = ³/₄ cup milk and ¹/₃ cup butter or margarine (only for use in cooking and baking)

Cream, light, 1 cup (in cooking or baking) = ³/₄ cup milk and 3 tablespoons butter or margarine or 1 cup evaporated milk

Egg, 1 whole egg = ¹/₄ cup egg substitute (like Egg Beaters, Scramblers, etc.) = 2 egg yolks = 2 egg whites

Flour, All-purpose white, 1 cup =¹/₂ cup whole wheat flour plus ¹/₂ cup all-purpose flour

Flour, cake, 1 cup = 1 cup minus 2 tablespoons all-purpose flour

Garlic, 1 clove = ¹/₈ teaspoon garlic powder

Herbs, fresh, 1 tablespoon = 1 teaspoon dry herbs

Lemon juice, 1 teaspoon = ¹/₂ teaspoon vinegar

Milk, whole, 1 cup =1 cup skim milk plus 2 tablespoons butter or 1 cup soy milk

Sour cream, 1 cup (for baking) = 1 cup yogurt

Sugar, Confectioner's, 1 cup = 1 cup granulated sugar processed in a food processor with 1 tablespoon cornstarch until powdery

Tomatoes = same amount of canned tomatoes

Tomato sauce, 1 cup = 6 tablespoons tomato paste and 1/2 cup water

Wine, red or white = same amount of pure red or white grape juice (in desserts) = same amount of chicken broth (in savory dishes)

COMMON COOKING TERMS

al dente: cooked just long enough to be firm rather than soft

bake: to cook in an oven using dry heat

barbecue: to cook food on a grill outdoors

baste: to moisten meat or fish with a liquid such as melted fat or cooking juices during the cooking process

beat: to mix moist ingredients vigorously in order to combine them, make them smooth, or incorporate air into them

blend: to mix different substances together so that they do not readily separate

boil: to cook something by submerging it in a boiling liquid for a certain amount of time

braise: to cook food, especially meat or vegetables, by browning briefly in hot fat, adding a little liquid, and cooking at a low temperature in a covered pot

broil: to cook food using direct heat

brown: to cook something in a frying pan, usually meat, until the exterior becomes brown

caramelize: to heat sugar until it turns dark brown; also, to cook fruit or vegetables until their natural sugars turn brown

cream: to mix ingredients—usually fat and sugar—with a spoon or electric mixer until soft and smooth

deglaze: to dissolve small particles of cooked food remaining in a skillet by adding a liquid and heating

dice: to cut into very small, usually square, pieces (1/8 to 1/4 inch)

drain: to remove liquid from a food

dredge: to coat food lightly with flour, sugar, or another substance

fry: to cook in hot fat (cooking in a small amount of fat is called pan-frying or sautéing; deep-frying is when fried foods are completely submerged in hot fat)

grease: to apply fat to a surface of a pan to prevent food from sticking

mince: to cut into very fine particles

parchment paper: a grease- and heat-resistant paper used to line baking pans or wrap food that is to be baked

preheat: to heat an oven, griddle, or broiler to the appropriate temperature before beginning to cook

puree: to blend food in an electric blender or food processor or press through a food mill to make a smooth, thick mixture

reduce: to cook a liquid to reduce its volume and concentrate its flavor

roast: to cook meat in an oven, uncovered, without additional liquid

sauté: to cook or brown in a small amount of fat

scald: to heat milk to just below the boiling point; also, to pour boiling water over food, or dip food briefly in boiling water

simmer: to cook slowly in a liquid just below the boiling point, generally over low heat

spread: to apply a mixture to a surface

springform pan: a circular baking pan with a separate bottom and sidewall held together with a clamp, which is released to free the baked product

steam: to cook food in steam, on a rack or in a steaming basket that has been placed inside a covered pan over boiling water

stew: to cook food slowly in simmering liquid in a covered pan

toss: to mix ingredients lightly with a lifting motion

whip: to beat rapidly with a wire whisk or electric mixer, incorporating air to lighten a mixture and increase its volume

whisk: to beat rapidly with a wire whisk until blended

zest: the thin, colored outer layer of a citrus peel

Seeing is deceiving.
It's eating that's believing.

James Thurber

INDEX

INDEX

INDEX

The authors would like to thank all the cooks and bakers in their lives who contributed to this book: Pleasance Coggershall, Kelly and Saxon Cote, Kate DeWitt, Lenore Dolan, Martin Fried, Marilyn Friedman, Marty Froese, Carolyn Goldman, Maren Gregerson, Marsha Heckman, Christopher Idone, Naomi Irie, Zena Katz, Hristo and Raddy Kolev, Jeffrey McCord, Anna Ostblöm, Philip Patrick, Marty Perlmutter, Sasha Perlraver, Frank Rehor, Linda Sunshine, Diana van Buren, Mary Vanderford, Clark Wakabayashi, Andrea Webber, Alice Wong

Published in 2006 by Welcome Books®
An imprint of Welcome Enterprises, Inc.
6 West 18th Street
New York, NY 10011
(212) 989-3200; Fax (212) 989-3205
www.welcomebooks.com

Publisher: Lena Tabori
Project Manager: Natasha Tabori Fried
Designer: Naomi Irie
Editorial Assistant: Maren Gregerson

Copyright © 2006 by Welcome Enterprises, Inc.

Library of Congress Cataloging-in-Publication Data

Fried, Natasha.
 The little big book of comfort food / by Natasha Tabori Fried, Katrina Fried, and Lena Tabori.
   p. cm.
 Includes bibliographical references and index.
 ISBN 1-59962-014-6 (hardcover : alk. paper)

1. Cookery. I. Fried, Katrina. II. Tabori, Lena. III. Title.
TX714.F745 2006
641.5--dc22

2006010997

ISBN-10: 1-59962-014-6
ISBN-13: 978-1-59962-014-5

Printed in China

First Edition

10 9 8 7 6 5 4 3 2 1

Art Credits:
Pg. 10: Gilette; Pg. 24: J. H. Buffords Sons; Pg. 35: Frances Brundage; Pg. 36: Carmichael; Pg. 50: Testu & Messin; Pg. 52: M. Vanasex; Pg. 59: Clay & Richmond; Pg. 70: MB; Pgs. 94, 156: Tom Browne; Pg. 96: E. Kreidolf; Pg. 101: Lawson Wood; Pg. 108: C. N. Morris; Pg. 130: Swift & Company; Pg. 137: Anne Anderson; Pgs. 140, 295: Ketterlinus; Pg. 168: Frank Hari; Pg. 177: Maxfield Parrish; Pg. 197: Ellen H. Clapsidille; Pg. 220: Raphael & Sons; Pg. 239: Lith H. Sicard & Farradesche; Pg. 245: Caiger & Jackson; Pg. 250: Starling; Pg. 271: Malick; Pg. 284: O. Merford; Pg. 306: Harry Rountree; Pg. 307: E Curtis; Pg. 308: Torre Bevaus; Pg. 317: L. R. Conwell; Pg. 324: C. Twelretrey; Pg. 336: Lucile Patterson; Pg. 340: A. Gammius Boecker